CW01183301

Colour
A Visual History

For Flora

An Hachette UK Company
www.hachette.co.uk

First published in the United Kingdom in 2019
by ILEX, a division of Octopus Publishing Group Ltd
Octopus Publishing Group, Carmelite House,
50 Victoria Embankment, London, EC4Y 0DZ
www.octopusbooks.co.uk

Text © Alexandra Loske 2019
Design and layout © Octopus Publishing Group 2019

Publisher: Alison Starling
Editorial Director: Helen Rochester
Commissioning Editor: Zara Larcombe
Managing Editor: Rachel Silverlight
Assistant Editor: Stephanie Hetherington
Art Director: Ben Gardiner
Designer: Luke Bird
Picture Research: Jennifer Veal
Senior Production Manager: Katherine Hockley

Ilex are proud to partner with Tate in our publishing programme; supporting the gallery in its mission to promote public understanding and enjoyment of British, modern and contemporary art.

All rights reserved. No part of this work may be reproduced or utilised in any form or by any means, electronic or mechanical, including photocopying, recording or by any information storage and retrieval system, without the prior written permission of the publisher.

Alexandra Loske asserts the moral right to be identified as the author of this work.

ISBN 978-1-78157-399-0

A CIP catalogue record for this book is available from the British Library

Printed and bound in China

10 9 8 7 6 5 4

Above: A twenty-first century colour globe by artist Eva Bodinet, inspired by the ideas of A. H. Munsell and Philipp Otto Runge.

Colour
A Visual History

Alexandra Loske

Contents

6 Introduction

Unravelling the Rainbow:
The Eighteenth-Century Colour Revolution

14 Isaac Newton Presents the Rainbow
16 Taking Up the Challenge: Colour After Newton
20 Allegorical and Figurative Images of Colour
24 J. C. Le Blon and the Trichromatic System
26 Moses Harris: Colours for the Natural World
30 The Beautiful and the Sublime
32 The Picturesque Palette
34 Colourmen: Apothecaries for Painters
36 The 'Lost Secret' of Venetian Colouring:
   A Woman Fools the Art Establishment

Romantic Ideas and New Technologies:
The Early Nineteenth Century

42 Darkness and Light: Goethe Challenges Newton
46 Observing Newton in the Garden
48 Reading Colour: William Oram's Memorandums
50 Mary Gartside's Abstract Colour Blots
54 Popular Manuals for Amateur Painters
56 A Taxonomy of Colours: *Werner's Nomenclature*
60 George Field: Science, Art and Symbolism
68 Instructive Palettes in Painters' Manuals
72 The 'Painter's Compass': Colour Wheels for Artists
74 Rudolph Ackermann Colours Fashionable Society
78 Frank Howard Breaks Down the Masters
82 Colour, Light and Shade: Turner's *Deluge* Paintings

Industrialism to Impressionism:
The Later Nineteenth Century

90 Into Darkness: M. E. Chevreul's Beautiful Science
100 From Science into Art: Chevreul and the
    Birth of Impressionism
102 A Poet's Philosophical Colour Categories
104 A Woman Travels in Search of Colour
106 George Barnard Cuts Up Pages
112 Trees and Butterflies Represent Latest Colour Advances
114 Ornamental Colour for Cosmopolitan Tastes
118 Immaterial to Material: Bridging the Gap
    between Science and Art
122 Vincent van Gogh Immerses Himself in Colour
124 Palettes as Mirrors: Artists and Their Colours
130 A Rose for Chevreul: Charles Lacouture's
    Répertoire chromatique

Colour for Colour's Sake:
The Radical Early Twentieth Century
138 Blots and Grids: Emily Noyes Vanderpoel
140 Albert Henry Munsell's Hue, Value and Chroma
146 Beyond Newton's Disc: New Ideas in Popular Manuals
154 Martin Fischer's Decaying Palette
156 Orphism: Colourful Music and Musical Colour
158 Mystical Colours: Hilma af Klint and Charles Leadbeater
162 From Blue to Infinity: Wassily Kandinsky and the Forms of Colours
166 Science and Maths in a Complex Colour System
170 Paul Klee and the 'Chromatic Keyboard'
174 Bauhaus: Minimalist Colour in Art and Design
176 The Art of Colour: Theory and Phenomenon
182 Psychological Colour for the Modern Home
186 Practical and Beautiful: The Art of Colour Printing
190 A Colour Dictionary: The Villalobos *Colour Atlas*

Colour into the Future:
The Wheels Keep on Spinning
196 Simple and Pictorial: A Children's Guide to Printing
198 Robert Francis Wilson and the Post-War Workspace
202 Accent on Colour: A Bold New Palette
204 'This is Colour Surprise': Popular Art Manuals in 1950s and '60s America
208 Parsons' *Tint Book* Revisited
210 Stained Glass: New Church Architecture
216 Sky and Sea: Colour Wheels for the Natural World
218 The Rainbow Lives On: Newton's Legacy in Contemporary Art and Culture
224 Falling Back in Love with Colour
226 Pantone® Sets a Colour Standard

228 Glossary
230 Bibliography
234 Index
238 Picture Credits
240 Acknowledgements

INTRODUCTION

Introduction

> *The order of colour, both practically and conceptually, is a mirror of its time*

Above: 'C' for 'Colour' from a fourteenth-century illuminated manuscript.

Left: Gabriele Münter's *Beim Malen (wohl Marianne von Werefkin)*, 1911.

This book charts the journey of colour exploration, expression and discovery through painters' tools, art, printed ephemera and literature. Throughout history, artists, scientists and philosophers have attempted to explain and picture the order of the visible colour spectrum. The order of colour, both practically and conceptually, is a mirror of its time as well as the person who created it, and is of universal aesthetic appeal.

For artists working with material colour, the order of colour has had a particularly practical context: Where to place which colour, on the palette as well as on the painting? How do colours influence each other, when physically mixed or optically juxtaposed? How to ensure you use an attractive or harmonious balance of colours on the canvas? An artist's palette is largely influenced by the medium the artist works in, where he or she works and by the kind of artists' materials that are available at the time, but it is also an expression of personal taste, style and the greater cultural context. Palettes and paint boxes can be the key that unlocks lost knowledge about colour and how it was prepared and used. One of the earliest surviving paint boxes, used by the Vizier Amenemope of Egypt in c.1427–1401 BCE, is a simple box with five pigments pressed into carved indentations: two types of carbon black, a mixed green pigment, blue frit and a red ochre. Despite, or even because of, its small size and simplicity, the box paints a vivid picture of the pigments available nearly three and a half thousand years ago.

Palettes also help us understand how and when artists mixed their colours, and how much they knew about pigments. The illustration of the initial 'C' for Colour in a fourteenth-century English manuscript (above left) tells us much about colour mixing and tools in the Middle Ages: each colour is kept in a separate dish and appears to be bright and premixed. More recent surviving painters' palettes can reveal how artists prepared the colour composition of a specific painting: whether they worked outdoors on first sketches can be gathered from the size of a paint box and the medium; the selection of paints in the box and any traces of mixed paints left on the inside of a tin or the surface of a palette can tell us what pigments were available or popular, as well as how they were mixed and applied.

When painters include palettes in self-portraits or portraits of other artists, the physical object is then given a symbolical meaning, reflecting the person's character and artistic style, as can clearly be seen in a portrait by Gabriele Münter from 1911 (opposite). It likely depicts another Expressionist painter, Marianne von Werefkin, with whom Münter shared a passion for primary colours freed from representational constraints, arranged here almost like a collage for maximum brilliancy. This attitude to colour is reflected perfectly in the sitter's palette included in the portrait, which she is holding at a slight angle, allowing the viewer to see how it is arranged. The painting is a

The predominantly abstract nature of colour gives these images a timeless and universal quality

carefully balanced composition in which the physical palette serves almost as a business card and signifier of artistic preferences.

From the early eighteenth century onwards, many colour systems and diagrams were designed and applied in both the arts and sciences. They are frequently depicted as a circular shape, such as this relatively simple hand-coloured colour wheel (opposite) by British artist Robert Arthur Wilson. Wilson published it privately in the 1920s to illustrate his ideas about colour order in relation to musical harmonies. Other diagrams are more fanciful and experimental, in the shape of triangles, diamonds or stars, or attempting three dimensions with 'colour globes', pyramids and cubes. Some of the earliest diagrams are simply lists of colours, usually intended to provide a resource for the reproduction or identification of colours, or an attempt towards standardisation.

Changing ideas about colour and the way we see it illustrated also reflect developments in print culture and technology, developing from uncoloured to hand-coloured plates, moving on to aquatinting and lithography, and further to photographic reproduction, large-scale silk screen-printing and eventually digital colour systems in the more recent past. The kinds of publications we find these images in also tells us much about the use and understanding of colour in certain times: when we see more art and theory books aimed at children and the general public, we know then that the populace was educated, and had access to painting materials and leisure time for hobbies.

Although this book is arranged in roughly chronological order, it is by no means a definitive history of colour systems or colour theory. It aims rather to celebrate the visual quality and beauty of colour systems and concepts, and to showcase the creativity with which these have been devised. Many of the diagrams shown here are well known in the canon of historic colour literature, but I have made a point of including several less familiar examples that complete the picture and may provide a few surprises. The same applies to art, especially from the late nineteenth century onwards, that directly addresses colour order and colour theory. Some very famous and popular works are represented here alongside lesser-known and recent examples, all of them underlining the continued interest and development of ideas about colour.

Wherever possible, I have tried to show the visuals in the context in which they were published, whether as illustrations in a bound book or in other formats. Some of these publications show signs of heavy use in libraries and artists' studios, which makes them even more evocative. The predominantly abstract nature of colour gives these images a timeless and universal quality that connects scientific, artistic and philosophical ideas expressed centuries apart. A colour wheel by Moses Harris from the 1770s resonates easily with colour ideas applied by the Bauhaus group to interior decoration, furniture and toys in the 1920s, as well as with a 360-degree walkway of rainbow colours created on top of a Danish art museum by Olafur Eliasson in 2011.

Opposite: Robert Arthur Wilson's hand-coloured educational colour circle in a 1920s pamphlet had an movable overlay to help artists create harmonious colour combinations.

THE COLOUR CIRCLE

SCHEME of COLOURS

Unravelling the Rainbow: The Eighteenth-Century Colour Revolution

The eighteenth century was a period of great intellectual, scientific and artistic ambition. The study of colour was one among many subjects of interest, but in just the first decade of the century two things happened that changed the field forever.

Sometime around 1706, the German chemist Heinrich Diesbach, working with the alchemist Johann Konrad Dippel, invented a new pigment called Prussian blue. This deep, rich blue based on an iron compound is often considered to be the first modern colour: that is, an inorganic and chemically produced pigment. It was a good alternative to the expensive mineral pigment ultramarine, and its invention heralded

> *By splitting white light, Newton identified the visible range of colours, or the rainbow spectrum*

the beginning of the commercial and large-scale production of a range of new pigments. This advancement would ultimately lead to good-quality colour becoming more affordable and available – not only for artists but also for any industry that worked with pigments.

The other, slightly earlier, event was the publication of a book. In 1704 the English scientist Isaac Newton published his *Opticks*, the comprehensive result of many years of researching light and colour.

By splitting white light, Newton identified the visible range of colours, or the rainbow spectrum. In *Opticks*, he built a colour system around his findings, and he visualised this system in a circular shape, making it one of the first printed colour wheels, albeit an uncoloured one. Attempts towards an objective colour system had been made before, but this was a substantial and hugely influential model based on decades of scientific experiments. Newton demonstrated the relationship between light and colour, and convincingly argued for a certain number of 'pure' hues that might provide the basis for a standardised colour system.

Newton's ideas were quickly disseminated, discussed and promoted in European intellectual circles. Soon other researchers began to create colour diagrams that would prove useful to the sciences and the arts. Many authors of colour treatises were indeed scientists as well as artists, or poets as well as scientists. A surprising number of writers on colour were botanists, geologists or entomologists, which might partly explain a heightened interest in accurate colour representation. This was certainly the case with the British entomologist Moses Harris, who included colour wheels, such as the one shown opposite, in his illustrated books on insects in the 1770s and even wrote a short, illustrated treatise just about colour. Almost all images in printed publications on colour were copperplate engravings or wood cuts. In the later eighteenth century, more and more of these images were coloured, but hand-colouring was still the only way to ensure accuracy in depicting colour systems or colour charts.

What unites most colour literature from the eighteenth century is an approach to colour theory based on science, investigation and the search for

Left: A colour wheel from Moses Harris's *Exposition of English Insects*, based on the various hues commonly found in the insects of Britain. Such a tool would probably have been used for accurately representing and identifying tints in the natural world.

OPTICKS:
OR, A
TREATISE
OF THE
REFLEXIONS, REFRACTIONS,
INFLEXIONS and COLOURS
OF
LIGHT.
ALSO
Two TREATISES
OF THE
SPECIES and MAGNITUDE
OF
Curvilinear Figures.

LONDON,

Printed for SAM. SMITH, and BENJ. WALFORD, Printers to the Royal Society, at the *Prince's Arms* in St. *Paul*'s Church-yard. MDCCIV.

colour systems and schematic representations, reflecting Enlightenment values. These diagrams were designed with the aims of clarity and instructive usefulness. Their format ranged from colour charts and lists to various geometric shapes, with the circle or wheel dominating.

For centuries, the rainbow had been used in art, mainly as a symbolically charged trope in both landscape painting and portraiture, often with little regard for optical accuracy. The post-Newtonian era saw a shift in the style of the rainbows and other figurative representations of colour, with a much greater emphasis on scientific accuracy.

Perhaps the most surprising thing was that the subject of colour was becoming popular and accepted in academic discussion. For centuries it had been considered inferior in the hierarchy of the elements of art. By the end of the eighteenth century, however, colour had become a standard element in aesthetic discourse, teaching and academic publications, although *colore* had not quite achieved the same status as *disegno* (line drawing).

Between 1769 and 1790, the President of the Royal Academy in London, Sir Joshua Reynolds, delivered lectures at the recently founded institution, in which he still discussed colour cautiously and predominantly in the context of the Italian masters, and even then only as a subordinate element in the art of painting. However, a change was coming. The influence of Newton and his followers, combined with the invention of many new pigments as well as watercolours in moist cake form, had made painting with colour an exciting occupation not just for serious artists but also for a much wider audience. The colour revolution had begun.

Left: Newton's colour circle, the diminutive and deceptively simple diagram marked 'Fig. 11', which is shown on a fold-out sheet in *Opticks*.

UNRAVELLING THE RAINBOW – THE EIGHTEENTH-CENTURY COLOUR REVOLUTION

Isaac Newton Presents the Rainbow

The most influential book on colour published in the eighteenth century was Isaac Newton's *Opticks: A Treatise of the Reflexions, Refractions, Inflections and Colours of Light*. First published in 1704 in English, when Newton was at the height of his fame, it was translated into a Latin edition in 1706 and went into many further editions in several other languages, and remained the focus of intellectual discussion and criticism in the field of colour studies until well into the nineteenth century.

Newton had bought his first prism in the early 1660s and begun experimenting on a serious level in 1666 while he was Professor of Mathematics at the University of Cambridge. He presented the results of his *experimentum crucis* (crucial experiment) of splitting white light into colours in the *Philosophical Transactions of the Royal Society* as early as January 1671. A sketch by Newton (opposite) illustrates the setup of his experiment, and provides the first image of white light being refracted into the visible spectrum. Although he eventually identified seven colours – red, orange, yellow, green, blue, indigo and violet – he noted only five in this sketch (initially, orange and violet were omitted). Newton also proved that these colours could be considered 'pure' (or what we might call primary), as they could not be split any further.

Newton envisaged colour in a deceptively simple-looking colour wheel, included in *Opticks* in the form of a copperplate illustration (see previous page). Handily, this plate folded out of the book so that readers could consult the illustration while reading the accompanying text. The seven colours he identified form the wheel like unequally carved slices of a cake, with the poles of the visible spectrum – red and violet – meeting at the axis marked with a D. Though the uncoloured circle does not immediately strike one as sophisticated, Newton was already making attempts at introducing a three-dimensional and mathematically quantifiable system, with the letters that mark the circle offering a means to describe the precise qualities of a specific colour. Notes in the text explain how the saturation of each colour increases from white at the centre, marked O, to its fullest saturation at the circumference. Additionally, Newton describes the mixing of the colours with their neighbours, so while the arch DE (for example) describes the colour red, we can imagine that red to be graded towards violet at point D and orange at point E, while the lower-case letters at the centre of each arch describe the colour's purest form.

The diagram includes an example of how it could be used. The circles above the lower-case letters of each segment represent different quantities of

---

The seven colours Newton identified form the wheel like unequally carved slices of a cake

---

coloured rays, for example, one ray for indigo and violet, through to ten rays for red, yellow and orange. From here, Newton calculated a common centre of all these colours, marked by the letter Z. Drawing the line OY, from centre to circumference, shows that the resulting compound will be a reddish orange, and since the Z is a little more than halfway down this line, the colour will be low intensity, with a lot of white light.

Above: Newton's early sketch of his *experimentum crucis* has only five distinct colours, rather than the seven he would finally settle on. By passing each coloured light through a second prism, as shown in this diagram, Newton showed that these spectral colours were 'pure', because this left them unchanged.

The usefulness of this wheel for artists or anyone working with material colour is not quite clear, since Newton was working with light – that is, with immaterial colour, also known as additive colour. While the spectrum of coloured light combines to create brighter, whiter light, mixing together the same range of colours in the form of paint would make for a darker, duller mixture. The wheel also places complementary colours opposite each other, as far as possible in an asymmetric design, but Newton did not elaborate on how this might affect the use of colour in art or design, something much discussed by later colour theorists.

The unequal division of the circle, with indigo and orange allotted much smaller segments, is another curiosity. An equally proportioned circle divided by an even number would make for a more aesthetically pleasing (and possibly more useful) diagram. Newton's aim, however was 'not to explain the Properties of Light by Hypotheses, but to propose and prove them by reason and experiment', making *Opticks* exemplary of the values of the Enlightenment.

Newton's colours do in fact represent the range of electromagnetic radiation, known as wavelength, that the human eye can see, despite the fact that the concept of wavelengths was not yet understood.

As for the seven colours identified on his wheel, like Pythagoras two millennia before him, Newton was making symbolic associations between music and colour. Each segment of his wheel relates to one of the seven diatonic intervals of the Doric mode, beginning and ending at D to form an octave. As we shall see, the notion that colour and music should be linked was explored later by many other colour writers and artists, well into the twentieth century, with abstract artists like Wassily Kandinsky and Robert and Sonia Delaunay exploring synaesthetic aspects of colour and music experience (see pages 156–157).

Although Newton's wheel drew criticism from contemporary and later thinkers, it was – and remains today – one of the most influential systems for ordering colour. If few people today can confidently differentiate indigo from blue, most any child will be familiar with the Newtonian acronym 'ROY G BIV'.

I. Ordnung der Farben claſſe.

XII. g. Feuerblau. I. gatt. Blau.

XI. g. Veilenblau. II. g. Meergrün.

X. g. Veilen roth. III. g. Grün.

IX. g. Karmaſinroth. IV. g. Oliven Grün.

VIII. g. Roth. V. g. Gelb.

VII. g. Feuerroth. VI. g. Oranien gelb.

Die Blühenden Farben.

Taking Up the Challenge: Colour After Newton

If Newton had set the challenge of how best to order colour, he would certainly not be the last to attempt a definitive, graphic system of colour. In 1708, the first known coloured images of colour circles (see overleaf) were published in Claude Boutet's *Traité de la peinture en mignature* on facing pages. The circles are decorated with pictorial scenes featuring putti and aristocratic ladies in genteel settings.

The first of the circles follows Newton's system: it is asymmetric and comprises seven colours – albeit now evenly proportioned. The second circle shows twelve colours and is symmetrical, perhaps to better illustrate the relationship between the colours – complementary colours in particular. In contrast to Newton's illustrations, they are coloured, by hand in watercolour, and the figurative scenes at the bottom of the page make it clear that the subject of work is material colour.

Newton's theory of colour was influential long after the publication of *Opticks*, and beyond his native tongue. The Austrian Jesuit priest and entomologist Ignaz Schiffermüller discussed why he supported Newton's theory in *Versuch eines Farbensystems (An attempt towards a system of colours)*, published in 1772. Where Newton proposed seven pure colours, however, Schiffermüller's colour wheel (left) comprised twelve: three primary, three secondary and six tertiary colours, each in equal 30-degree segments – like Boutet, changing Newton's asymmetric and unequally divided spectrum into a symmetrical system.

Schiffermüller applied his system strictly to material colour and the art of scientific illustration, yet he nevertheless paid tribute to Newton's experiments with the pictorial vignettes surrounding the circle, presenting painting, or the material application of colour, in the context of his scientific methods.

In the eighteenth century, some attempts were made at depicting colour systems in three dimensions. The aim of such schemas was to include other dimensions of colour, such as saturation or the light value of tints. Some of these early three-dimensional systems have triangular and pyramidal shapes, such as one proposed by the German astronomer and map-maker Tobias Mayer in 1758. He in turn influenced the German astronomer and mathematician Johann Heinrich Lambert, who interpreted and extended Mayer's numbered triangular system and presented a seven-tiered *Farbenpyramide* (colour pyramid) in 1772, containing 107 tints (below).

The topmost triangle represents 'whiteness or light', while the colours in the lowest triangle 'are mostly quite dark except where they border on yellow'. The pyramid sits on a base of twelve pigments, named in the text as Naples yellow, lamp black, king's yellow, juice green, auripigment, chrysocolla, azurite, verdigris, smalt, cinnabar, indigo and Florentine lake. These are twelve pigments (as opposed to colour names) that were commonly available in Germany in 1772, so apart from creating a conceptual diagram of colour, he was also providing practical advice on which pigments could be considered to resemble the colours outlined above. Lambert also provided a key for the 107 tints displayed in the tiers of the pyramid, thus stressing the applicability of his system to merchants and the dyeing industry, as well as artists, and placing his system firmly in the world of material colour.

Left: Ignaz Schiffermüller's colour wheel from 1772 pays homage to Newton's findings but proposes a more equally divided order, with twelve colours rather than seven.

Right: Johann Heinrich Lambert's *Farbenpyramide* was created the same year as Schiffermüller's circle. This colour pyramid places the primaries red, blue and yellow in the corners, with various combinations in between.

Left & right: In 1708, Claude Boutet produced what are believed to be the first coloured colour wheels in print. The one on this page appears to follow Newton's ordering, giving seven colours rather than the even-numbered, symmetric kind offered on the facing page. You will notice, however, that rather than the two kinds of blue proposed by Newton (indigo and blue), Boutet depicts two kinds of red: 'Rouge de Feu' (fire red) and 'Rouge Cramoisi' (crimson red).

18 UNRAVELLING THE RAINBOW – THE EIGHTEENTH-CENTURY COLOUR REVOLUTION

UNRAVELLING THE RAINBOW – THE EIGHTEENTH-CENTURY COLOUR REVOLUTION

Allegorical and Figurative Images of Colour

Even before Newton's colour theory had become part of the scientific vernacular, representations of colour and colour order often featured in paintings in the form of rainbows or palettes. They are seen most prominently in allegorical self-portraits depicting the art of painting or colouring, as in Giovanni Domenico Cerrini's *Allegory of Painting* (1639), opposite. Usually – as with Cerrini's example – Painting is represented by a woman holding palettes and brushes, or by putti or cupids playing with artists' tools, or combinations of these. In personifications of the art of painting or colour, artists often made visual and compositional references to colour order. The colours of the fabrics in this painting, for example, are all pure primaries: blue, yellow and red, plus green, which was often considered a primary. Associations of colour and the art of painting with women are likely to have their origins in Greek mythology, where the goddess Iris was the personification of the rainbow and a messenger of the gods. This also explains the clouds and skies in conjunction with colours and rainbows that make frequent appearances, especially in baroque and rococo painting.

Figurative and allegorical representations of colour continued to be published throughout the eighteenth century alongside abstract diagrams and charts. They appear to have had a popular appeal as affordable prints, as the case of Angelica Kauffman's *Colouring* suggests. Kauffman, a founding member of the Royal Academy in London and, incidentally, later a friend of Johann Wolfgang von Goethe, was commissioned in 1778 to produce ceiling roundels for the new Council Chamber in the Royal Academy when it was still located at Somerset House on the Strand, in London. The four roundels, painted in oil, depict the 'four elements of art': Design, Invention, Composition and Colour. Female allegorical figures are usually set in a neoclassical context; Kauffman's *Colouring* (see overleaf) depicts a female painter dipping her paintbrush into a Newtonian rainbow. A chameleon in the foreground offers a further allusion to colour. The images were stipple-engraved by Francesco Bartolozzi in 1787 and appear to have been some of the most popular prints after Kauffman, even though the engraving renders them black and white. The rainbow might here symbolise the painter's understanding of colour as relying on Newton's findings. Significantly, the colour scheme of the original painting is formed of dominant shades of the three primaries: red (in the woman's shawl or cape), yellow (her dress) and blue (the sky), all set against neutral naturalistic browns, greens and greys.

Intriguingly, the earliest description of the painting by Joseph Baretti in *A Guide Through the Royal Academy* from 1781 mentions a prism in place of the paint palette: '*Colouring* appears in the form of a blooming young Virgin, brilliantly, but not gaudily, dressed. The varied Colours of her garments unite and harmonise together. In one hand she holds a prism, in the other a brush, which she dips into the Tints of the Rainbow.' It is possible that the prism was painted

Associations of colour and the art of painting with women are likely to have their origins in Greek mythology

over at some point. Kauffman's fascination with the rainbow and, it can be assumed, the study of colour literature, was later echoed by the second president of the Royal Academy, Benjamin West, who as early as 1787 would advise his students to use the rainbow as a guiding principle in painting: 'in that point Nature has placed the most glowing colours of the Rainbow, so that any deviation from this order of colours becomes offensive, and sikens every Eye.'

The conflation of the symbols of contemporary colour theory and the material aspects of painting, combined with overt references to Newton, can also be seen in an anonymous print from the same period

Opposite: Giovanni Domenico Cerrini's *Allegory of Painting* (1639) is typical of seventeenth and eighteenth century artists' self-portraits. It features a female figure, representing Art, the painter's tools, and, prominently, the colours red, yellow, blue and green. A tetrachromatic order of colour was dominant at the time, meaning that green would likely have been viewed as a primary colour.

Above: Kauffman's image of *Colour* (1778–80) was hugely popular, showing how important colour and colour theory was becoming in the artworld. Previously, it had been treated as inferior to design and line drawing.

Above left: A print from 1785 featuring a painter's palette, as well as a prism, suggests the importance of Newton's theory for artists, despite the fact that it dealt with immaterial colour.

Above right: Detail of a print after George Romney, made just over a century after the publication of Newton's *Opticks*, shows how literal the depiction of colour theory had become by the nineteenth century.

entitled *Theory of Colours* (1785), above left. Here, the reference to Newton is made explicit by a female figure holding a prism against the sunlight, with the spectral colours appearing on what could be a large sketchbook or portfolio. Multiple pictorial references are made to painting and even the production of pigments: gathered on the table next to the figure are a painter's palette with paint brushes, a phial (most likely for the preparation of pure pigments), a book (an allusion to the theory underpinning painting) and flowers, which might represent the genre of flower painting or the imitation of nature in painting in general. A large vat in the background might be for pigment production or pigment storage. This small but significant engraving reflects the appreciation and status of colour studies and colour theory in the later eighteenth century and refers to their application in the fine arts and even pigment production.

Into the nineteenth century, figurative pictorial images of colour theory, optical concepts or the art of painting in general made way for much more literal and narrative illustrations. A number of decorative prints depicting Newton carrying out his experiments with prisms and light were produced throughout the nineteenth century, as for example a posthumously published print after George Romney entitled *Newton with the Prism* (1809), above. The scene is romanticised, showing Newton surrounded by scientific instruments and apparently performing his experiments with a prism in order to educate the two young women, possibly his niece and a maid, present; this perhaps being indicative of the association of the art of watercolour as a pastime for young ladies.

J. C. Le Blon and the Trichromatic System

Opposite: Apart from several plates illustrating the printing progress using the example of a portrait, Le Blon's book has a fold-out plate with the image of an actual painter's palette on which fifteen colour mixtures, discussed in a chapter on 'flesh colour', are shown. This is one of the earliest recorded instructive images of a painter's palette.

The exchange of ideas occurring within Europe during the eighteenth century is evident in the plethora of early translations of published works, the number of authors with a multicultural background or education, much cross-referencing in the works, and the occasional bilingual edition. J. C. Le Blon's *Coloritto*, or, *The Harmony of Colouring in Painting*/*L'Harmonie du coloris dans la peinture*, first published in London between 1723 and 1726 as a bilingual English/French edition, is an excellent example of this cosmopolitan attitude, as well as being an important early work on multicoloured printing technique.

Born in Frankfurt, Le Blon had studied in Rome and Switzerland and gained experience in his profession as an engraver and printer in Paris, London, Germany and Amsterdam. He was credited by the influential colour theorist Faber Birren as being responsible for initiating the prevalence of the trichromatic colour system. Older colour systems were frequently tetrachromatic – comprising four colours, usually red, yellow and blue, and black or green – although the concept of three primaries, as the basis for mixing all other hues, had been long known to artists.

Le Blon applied his system to printing, and invented a three-colour (and four-colour, with the addition of black) printing technique described in *Coloritto*, which could reproduce works of art with fair accuracy – far better than the black-and-white reproductions available at the time. He stated: 'Painting can represent all visible Objects, with three Colours, Yellow, Red, and Blue; for all other Colours can be compos'd of these Three, which I call Primitive.' The cost and resources required for such prints was, however, prohibitive, and Le Blon's model was unsuccessful, commercially at least.

But his method was well founded. Perhaps it helped that, unlike many of his contemporaries, Le Blon clearly understood the difference between subtractive and additive colour. In his short and now extremely rare publication, the author differentiates between the two, referencing Isaac Newton: 'I am only speaking of Material Colours, or those used by Painters; for a Mixture of all the primitive impalpable Colours, that cannot be felt, will not produce Black, but the very Contrary, White; as the Great Sir Isaac Newton has demonstrated in his *Opticks*.'

Première Planche

PRISMATIC

Moses Harris: Colours for the Natural World

In England it was the entomologist Moses Harris who produced the first comprehensive system of colours in his short publication *The Natural System of Colours* (c. 1769–1776). Harris's theory provides a good example of the muddling of additive and subtractive colour that was common throughout the eighteenth century. He explained: 'By the term colour, or colours, we would be understood to mean one or all of those appearances which are seen in the rainbow refracted by the prism, or that so beautifully decorate the leaves of flowers, or any other substance except such as are white, which is but a term for a total privation or absence of colour…' combining Newton's light-based colour theory with concepts of beauty in nature, as expressed by Edmund Burke and William Hogarth in the mid-eighteenth century. Despite the reference to Newton's experiment, his description of white as an absence of colour makes it clear that its application is subtractive, or material, colour.

Harris's system provided guidance for painters and pigment-makers, based on a principle of three primary colours or 'primitives' (red, yellow and blue), three 'mediates' (orange, green and purple), and their various combinations. He illustrated his work with copper plates showing two concentric circles, each comprising eighteen sectors of 'prismatic' and 'compound' colours at varying degrees of intensity, resulting in a total of 660 different tints. The overlapping triangles of primaries and secondaries sit prominently in the centre of each circle. As this system could not be adequately represented by the mechanical colouring techniques available at the time, Harris himself engraved the copper plates and hand-coloured them, using pigments such as red lead, which was one of the earliest pigments to be created artificially – it can be found in medieval manuscripts, and is still in use today. Some of the colours in surviving copies of the first edition have deteriorated badly, showing black splotches on the colour wheels, most likely caused by delayed chemical reaction of mixed pigments and painting materials.

We don't know exactly what inspired Harris to produce his concise book on colour, but it is most likely that he saw the need for a practical and precise guide to the use of colour in scientific illustrations. Before colour photography, such illustrations would have been essential for the reliable description and identification of natural forms. His much larger publications on the insects of Britain are lavishly illustrated with meticulously coloured plates, showing the exact colouring of flies, moths, beetles and butterflies. In one of these books, *Exposition of English Insects*, he applied his colour wheel to the specific purpose of representing the many shades of brown, grey and black found in insects (see page 10). Like Newton's wheel in *Opticks*, it can be seen as a colour guide for the figurative illustrations in the books. In the accompanying text he addresses the responsibility of the artist to use his or her professional judgement when producing tints. He also includes an explanatory key to the tints in the circle, which names and describes the colours shown in it.

In true Enlightenment spirit, accuracy in depicting the natural world was of utmost importance to Harris, and his colour wheels were nothing less than complex tools with which to achieve this. The fact that the colour wheel plate is often missing in copies of *Exposition* might indicate that many of his readers removed it from the book block to consult alongside the other plates.

Left & overleaf: Moses Harris's colour wheels show a 'prismatic' range (left) of eighteen hues, based on the primaries red, blue and yellow, and their immediate combinations, and 'compound' colours (overleaf), based on orange, green and purple, and their combinations.

6

PRISMATIC.

Red, orange-red, red-orange; orange, yellow-orange, orange-yellow; yellow, green-yellow, yellow-green; green, blue-green, green-blue; blue, purple-blue, blue-purple; purple, red-purple, purple-red.

COMPOUND.

Orange, olave-orange, orange-olave; olave, green-olave, olave-green; green, slate-green, green-slate; slate, purple-slate, slate-purple; purple, brown-purple, purple-brown; brown, orange-brown, brown-orange.

If the colours were divided into a still greater number of teints or divisions, which it is conceived is all that can be done in attempting to improve the system, it would not render it more useful, but rather tend to create confusion between the teints which are now just sufficiently conspicuous, and would be one step toward reducing it to the chaos from which the author has taken so much pains to extricate it.

In contrasting colours, so frequently necessary in various branches of painting, this work will be found of great use; for if a contrast is wanting to any colour or teint, look for the colour or teint in the system, and directly opposite you will find the contrast wanted; viz. suppose it is required to know what colour is most opposite, or contrary in hue, to red; look directly opposite to that colour in the system, and it will be found to be green, which is the compound of the two other primitives: the most contrary to blue is orange, and opposite to yellow is purple;

COMPOUND

The Beautiful and the Sublime

Above: Although the palette diagram makes up just a tiny part of this plate from Hogarth's *Analysis of Beauty* (1753), its position at the top and centre certainly affords it some importance.

Opposite: With several brushes in one hand and a palette knife in the other, Hogarth displays the apparatus of his trade. Holding his palette up to provide a full-frontal view of its surface, the spectrum of 'original' tints stands out on a canvas that is coloured mainly in tertiary hues.

Most of the colour manuals published in the eighteenth century were concerned with painting techniques and how to prepare paints and apply surface finishes. Robert Dossie's *The Handmaid to the Arts* was one of the most popular books of this kind. First published in London in 1758, it went into numerous revised and enlarged editions up until 1829. The enduring demand for Dossie's *Handmaid* and similar publications might have been influenced by the increased promotion of the arts in Britain from the mid-eighteenth century onwards. These technical handbooks rarely mentioned colour theory beyond basic principles of colour mixing.

A number of artists and philosophers were, however, expressing views on colour in relation to aesthetic ideas of beauty and 'the sublime'. While beauty was considered a standard that could be identified, measured and even created, the concept of the sublime described a more elusive reaction; an impression of grandeur, awe and fear. It encompassed things that were both fascinating and threatening, impressive and untameable, for example vast mountain ranges, storms and darkness. Especially later in the eighteenth century we see this reflected in large-scale paintings of alpine landscapes, disasters at sea, storms or biblical scenes such as Noah and the Flood.

Edmund Burke was one such thinker who included a chapter on 'Colour considered as productive of the sublime' in his *A Philosophical Inquiry Into the Origin of Our Ideas of the Sublime and Beautiful* (1757). He advocated darkness and gloom in painting and architecture and advised against gaudiness induced by colour: 'The cloudy sky is more grand than the blue; and night is more sublime and solemn than day.'

Not so, however, for Burke's contemporary, the painter William Hogarth. Hogarth was strongly influenced by Isaac Newton's *Opticks*, and possibly also by a painting manual by Dutch painter Gérard de Lairesse, published in English with the title *The Art of Painting* in 1735. Like Newton and Lairesse, Hogarth embraced the concept of pure prismatic colours. He disliked darkness and shadows in painting, despite sometimes considering them necessary. In his privately published treatise on taste *The Analysis of Beauty* (1753) he proclaimed that '[t]here are but three original colours in painting besides black and white, viz. red, yellow and blue. Green, and purple, are compounded … however these compounds being so distinctly different from the original colours, we will rank them as such.' He applied this five-colour system to an artist's palette, even including it in one of the instructive fold-out plates that illustrate *Analysis of Beauty* (above). The palette image is only a small part of a much larger, uncoloured etching, but there is some detail, with the blots being graded and numbered to indicate seven degrees of brightness and permanency.

For Hogarth, the palette had a symbolic significance. He included painters' tools in several of his self-portraits, often placing them prominently in the composition. In his self-portrait from 1757 (above), we see him sitting in a chair, looking at a large canvas, about to start painting. The palette forms the focal point of the painting, linking the artist with the canvas spatially and symbolically. The tints on the palette are arranged along the outer edge and consist of six bright colours, more or less resembling his system of a few pure tints from which all others can be created. There is an additional blot of white nearest to the thumbhole, and no sign of blacks, browns or greys. Here is Hogarth putting his ideas about colouring into practice, holding his palette up like a trade card.

The Picturesque Palette

The later eighteenth century saw a dramatic rise in the popularity of the medium of watercolour, linked to the invention of solid, soluble watercolour cakes by William Reeves in *c.* 1780, making it easy for artists to carry a range of colours in compact form and paint *en plein air* or while travelling. While mid-eighteenth century aesthetic ideas were split between the contrasting concepts of the beautiful and the sublime, a third way later arose that sought to combine the ideals of both. This new vision of nature known as the 'picturesque' may have been made possible simply because more artists were able to paint outdoors, farther afield and in remote places, and spend time actually observing their subject.

Around 1790 the English artist and author William Gilpin, one of the key proponents of the concept of the picturesque, included comments on a colour system based on three primaries in a notebook entitled *Hints to Form the Taste & Regulate ye Judgment in Sketching Landscape*. This was perhaps an early draft for his influential *Three Essays: On Picturesque Beauty, on Picturesque Travel and on Sketching Landscape*. Referring to landscape painting, he states: 'In order to colour chastely & Harmoniously, use only 3 Tints: Red, yellow, & Blue, of wh[ich] compose the other colours wh[ich] are requisite to make out the parts in the diff. distances.' On the facing page he sketched a colour chart illustrating tints that he recommended to achieve the appearance of certain levels of distance, alongside a small landscape sketch composed with these tints (right).

Gilpin's concern for colour 'chastity' and harmony is connected to picturesque ideals of a natural, 'rugged' beauty, but his dedication to a trichromatic system is exemplary of the heightened awareness and understanding of both basic principles of colour order and issues of pigment purity and colour mixing in the late eighteenth century. This is reiterated in print in *Three Essays* some years later (1792), to which Gilpin added a poem titled 'On Landscape Painting':

One truth she gives, that Nature's simple loom
Weaves but with three distinct, or mingled, hues,
The veil that cloaths Creation: These are red,
Azure, and yellow. Pure and unstain'd white
(If colour deem'd) rejects her gen'ral law,
And is by her rejected.
[...]
Draw then from these, as from three plenteous springs,
Thy brown, thy purple, crimson, orange, green,
Nor load thy pallet with a useless tribe
Of pigments, when commix'd with needful white,
As suits thy end, these native three suffice.

Left: A sketch from Gilpin's notebook from *c.* 1790, intended to show the use of colour in depicting distance. The greatest space is given to the hues that comprise the background as it recedes. On the facing page in his notebook, Gilpin added notes expounding on their use, including: 'Shadow of the clouds comprised of all the tints', 'Blue at the remotest distance' and 'The foreground of the same but deeper. On this, browns and greens to be laid to make out the parts.'

Colourmen: Apothecaries for Painters

Left: A portable watercolour box, produced and sold by Waring & Dimes, London in c. 1840, with the remains of watercolour cakes, among them chrome yellow, crimson lake and Prussian blue.

Above: Allen's 'colour-shop' in London, painted by George Scharf in 1829.

'Colourman' was a term for a person who either supplied pigments or assisted an artist in the messy and labour-intensive process of making pigments and preparing paints, varnishes and other materials. It is not known when exactly the term was first used, but professional colourmen appear to have been operating in England since at least the 1720s. In an overview of trades in London from 1747, the author, Richard Campbell, comments that the colourman 'is, in some shape, the Apothecary to the Painter', subtly comparing paint-making to alchemy. Extensive training and experience were necessary to become an established colourman, as Campbell explained: 'No Man is fit to keep a Colour-Shop who has not served an apprenticeship: The articles they deal in are so many, and require such a nice eye, and so great practice to be a judge of them, that even seven years are too little to learn this trade.'

Towards the end of the eighteenth century, the colour trade expanded significantly and many large-scale firms and shops were founded, manufacturing and selling a wide range of artists' materials, including newly invented watercolour cakes and portable artists' boxes. Some of these firms are still trading today, such as Reeves (founded by the Reeves brothers in 1766) and Rowney's (founded in 1783 by Richard and Thomas Rowney – now Daler-Rowney). Winsor & Newton, founded by the painters William Winsor and Charles Newton, were operating in London from 1832 and became one of the leading British art suppliers in the Victorian period.

George Scharf's painting from 1829 (above) of Edward Prascey Allen's shop in St. Martin's Lane in London is one of very few detailed images of a colour shop in the early nineteenth century. The exterior is brightly painted in green, and brushes, jars of paint and other painting materials are displayed prominently in the windows. Two men – probably a painter and his apprentice – are shown leaving the shop, laden with supplies, and inside the shop we can just about see the colourman grinding pigment. This real shop was conveniently located in the same building as 'Mrs Wats/Laydies School' – these ladies would almost certainly have received classes in painting in watercolour.

The 'Lost Secret' of Venetian Colouring: A Woman Fools The Art Establishment

A biting satire on the art establishment's gullibility and their obsession with colour in the 1790s

In this large (55 x 41 cm) and busy print (opposite) the satirist James Gillray mercilessly pokes fun at the British art establishment, such as it was at the end of the eighteenth century. The image is full of recognisable figures and details, and invites the viewer to look at it closely and discover ever more meanings. The full title of the print is *Titianus Redivivus; – or – The Seven-Wise-Men consulting the new Venetian Oracle*. The Latin part means 'Titian born again' – a reference to the Venetian painter Titian, known for his revolutionary use of colour in the sixteenth century. The central female figure balancing on a rainbow that is arching over the 'academic grove', representing predominantly the Royal Academy in London, is a woman called Ann Jemima Provis. Provis had just caused a storm in the art world by claiming that she had discovered an old manuscript detailing the secret of Titian's use of colour in painting. She offered this 'lost secret' to the Academy, but it was later discovered that she was a fraud. She holds a palette and brushes, wears a gown with a long train of peacock feathers and seems to reign supreme, but before her is a simple clay pot in which she crudely mixes her colours, in the manner of common sign-painters rather than distinguished artists.

The image is filled with speech bubbles of additional text that satirise the affair. Each of the painters in the first row is poised with a palette, brush and paint board, and the texts in their speech bubbles show how each of them were fooled by Provis's lies. 'Will this Secret make me Paint like Claude? – will it make a Dunce, a Colourist at once?' asks the painter on the far right, identifiable as Joseph Farington.

One who has already had access to part of the fake manuscript and hoping to benefit from it financially is the reigning President of the Royal Academy, the American Benjamin West, who can be seen among a small shadowy group in the foreground on the right. Fleeing the scene, he says to the printer Josiah Boydell: 'Charming Secret Friend, for thee to dash out another Gallery with! – but I'm off!!' In the bottom left corner we can see the late first President, Sir Joshua Reynolds, who had been cautious about elaborate use of colour in his teaching, turning in his grave, exclaiming: 'Black Spirits & White; Blue Spirits & Grey. Mingle, mingle, mingle! – you that Mingle may.'

The image is a highly entertaining and biting satire on the art establishment's gullibility and their obsession with colour in the 1790s. Its iconography uses familiar symbols and imagery of the theory and practice of colour and colouring, including rainbows, palettes and other artists' materials, all in an ironic manner. Gillray was perhaps inspired by Angelica Kauffman's ceiling roundel commissioned by the Royal Academy in 1778, in which a female figure representing colour is depicted dipping her brush into a rainbow (see page 22). Certainly, he would have had good inside knowledge of the institution he so fervently rejected: in the late 1770s he had studied there under the Italian engraver Francesco Bartolozzi – the same Bartolozzi responsible for the popular prints of Kauffman's roundels.

Opposite: This busy print by James Gillray from 1797 satirises the art establishment of the nineteenth century, embodied in London's Royal Academy.

TITIANUS REDIVIVUS;—or—The Seven-Wise-Men consulting the new Venetian Oracle,—a Scene in ye Academic Grove.

XII.

Newtonische Mucken und homogene Lichter

Romantic Ideas and New Technologies: The Early Nineteenth Century

Left: With this plate from *Farbenlehre* (1810–1812), Goethe subtly ridicules Newton's method of experimenting with small objects or creatures on pieces of paper to prove his theory of homogenous lights and colours. In his comments to the plate, Goethe accuses Newton of being random in his methodology and claims that he recreated Newton's experiment with coloured paper and could see a range of colours where darker and lighter shades meet.

The early nineteenth century saw a surge in painters' manuals and general publications on colour, as well as theoretical treatises. The reasons for this spanned ideas rooted both in Enlightenment thinking and in notions of beauty and composition taken from the Romantic movement. Scientists and artists alike were lecturing on colour, proposing colour theories and publishing practical colour manuals. In this period, the boundaries between these quite different fields were often blurred. Colour theories, charts and diagrams were also often embedded in books on interior design or painting manuals. In the nineteenth century, ideas from the seemingly disparate worlds of science, philosophy and the arts met in new and fruitful combinations. There was also significant cultural exchange among colour writers within Europe, manifested in the number of dual-language editions and early translations of books that were available.

Illustrating books on colour in colour remained costly and labour-intensive, as lithography – a new mechanical method of reproducing images – was still in its infancy. In the early years of the nineteenth century we find a curious and exciting variety of illustrations dealing with the difficult issue of conveying ideas and practical advice about colour in images. Some authors or publishers decided not to include colour illustrations, in order to make the books more affordable. Often plates were coloured by hand, for the all-important sake of accuracy, and books were then marketed as highly desirable and collectible objects in an attempt to appeal to bibliophiles. Other authors and publishers used a combination of methods, for example enhancing prints with hand-colouring, or giving the readers the option of purchasing either a coloured or uncoloured edition, according to the price they were willing to pay.

Many early-nineteenth-century colour writers focussed on themes such as light and shade, composition, colour harmony and contrast. Building on the concepts of the sublime and the picturesque developed throughout the eighteenth century, the prevalent aesthetic across the arts in the early nineteenth century was Romanticism. This new movement was partially a backlash against the ideals of rigid order, temperance, rationality and physical materialism imposed under the Classicist and Enlightenment modes of thinking that had previously dominated. In contrast, Romanticism emphasised darkness, chaos and mystery, the emotional and the subjective.

It is in the early years of the nineteenth century that we find a curious and exciting variety of illustrations

One of the leading authors on colour in this period was Johann Wolfgang von Goethe. Poet and playwright, novelist, scientist and statesman, Goethe exemplifies the pluralistic character of his time. His work meanwhile – the substantial and strongly anti-Newtonian treatise on colour *Zur Farbenlehre* – is equally representative of Romantic ideals in the themes with which it is preoccupied and its focus on subjective or psychological perception. Goethe's ideas not only characterise the period he lived through,

The Industrial Revolution was making everyone richer. With greater wealth came more leisure time

Opposite: The nineteenth century saw the popularisation of colour studies. Colour theory often played a prominent role in books for amateur painters. This illustration – the 'Painter's Compass' from 1826 – appears in a treatise on colour by artist and art teacher Charles Hayter and in many aspects develops further the ideas of Moses Harris.

but also remained important – and controversial – long after his death. His treatise may read more like a catalogue of phenomena than a theory – descriptive rather than analytical and scientifically applicable – but it had great influence on artists and philosophers; in the latter case pre-empting phenomenology.

At the same time, many other artists, scientists and writers were experimenting with colour and publishing on the subject, resulting in some of the most visually striking examples of illustrations in the history of print culture. Although the topic of colour was popular, and the creative and publishing output unprecedented, illustrated books remained expensive both to make and buy, and were therefore available only to a relatively small readership. This began to change around the late 1830s, when books on colour became significantly smaller in size and scale, utilising new reproduction methods, and thus appealing to a much wider readership. The same applied to painting materials. Smaller, cheaper and more convenient paint boxes, watercolour satchels, paint in collapsible tubes, and other artists' tools made painting out in the open or in cramped spaces easier and led to a sharp rise in the popularity of painting as a pastime.

At the same time as manufacturers were adapting to make their products available to the general populace, the growing availability of these items also reflects the changing social and economic situation in Europe. The Industrial Revolution that had begun in the second half of the eighteenth century was making everyone richer. With greater wealth came more leisure time, and a new social strata – the middle class – arrived to make the most of it. Amateur painting, naturalism and outdoor pursuits flourished, as did general interest in academia. Colour was a popular topic for the public in a similar way to the pop-science books of today.

In the nineteenth century we also see how the concept of interior design develops as a distinct art form. Apart from house-painters' and decorators' manuals and high-end publications depicting grand interiors, magazines that gave advice on colours and fabrics for soft furnishings became fashionable. The lists of available colours and the fabric samples provided in the London fashion magazine *The Repository of Arts, Literature, Commerce, Manufactures, Fashions and Politics* by Rudolph Ackermann are not so different from the colour charts that can be picked up in DIY stores today. It was the beginning of the commercialisation of colour.

PLATE. 2. THE PAINTERS COMPASS.

Darkness and Light: Goethe Challenges Newton

German polymath Johann Wolfgang von Goethe was interested in many aspects of the sciences, including botany and geology. He had begun experimenting with colour in the 1780s, and published treatises on colour as early as 1791–92, including *Beyträge zur Optik (Contributions to Optics)*, in which he proposed a dualistic colour system based on the polarity of darkness and light, represented by the 'pure' colours blue and yellow, from which all other colours derived, including red. Goethe argued that black and white were not colours as such, but instead representations of total darkness and the brightest light:

> ... hence pure white represents light, while pure black represents darkness, and in the manner in which we call prismatic appearance colour, black and white cannot be considered colours; but there are black-and-white pigments, which allow the appearance to be seen on objects.

In true empirical spirit, readers of *Beyträge zur Optik* were encouraged to recreate certain experiments with three-sided prisms, often involving looking through a prism at various objects and surfaces. For this purpose Goethe included an expensively produced set of 27 woodblock-printed and coloured 'playing cards' with the publication.

Goethe pursued his research into colour for a further twenty years, culminating in what was probably the most substantial treatise on colour composed in the nineteenth century. *Zur Farbenlehre* (literally: *On the Doctrine of Colours*) was published in three volumes between 1810 and 1812. Despite all his significant publications of literature and poetry, he considered this large work on many aspects of colour perception, creation, meaning and application his most important intellectual achievement. His intention was to not just present another colour system but to link colour to many aspects of science, art, design and psychology, and put his study into the wider context of the history of colour writings. The sheer volume of text in *Farbenlehre* is partly explained by Goethe's observational style. Where Newton was devoted to objective scientific theory, Goethe's approach reflected the times he lived in: subjective and physiological perceptions, rooted in human experience, were no less important than Newton's rationally proven 'facts'. The observations Goethe collected focus on the various phenomena of colour, including impressions of after-images, contrast effects of colour on the appearance of other colours, and the effect of colour on the appearance of size ('[b]lack dresses make people seem smaller than light ones'), for example. These observations at least have the benefit of being backed up by his experiments. Later he goes on to discuss purely subjective moral, psychological and cultural associations with colour.

The third volume includes sixteen coloured plates, several of them consisting of multiple images. Not many of the images show diagrams that order colour in a logical and practically transferable system, but they do illustrate the number and complexity of Goethe's observations.

Goethe attempted to disprove Newton's colour theories by recreating some of his prismatic experiments. In the 'Polemic part' of his *Farbenlehre*, he questions and tests the validity of Newton's research methods and findings. Goethe's main argument against Newton concerned the creation of colour. While Newton had proven that, in certain contained circumstances – namely a darkened room and one directed ray of pure sunlight – the visible colour spectrum appears (at a certain distance) as a refraction of that ray of light, Goethe argued that these were unnatural circumstances. His own theory was that colour was created at the point where darkness and light meet. He supported this theory with the playing cards in his first publication and similar illustrations to his *Farbenlehre*. Anyone, he claimed, could look at his illustrations of black-and-white geometrical shapes through a prism, in ordinary light conditions, and see colour appear on the edges and fringes. He also included a number of coloured copperplate engravings illustrating the failings of Newton's methods in the collection of plates accompanying his *Farbenlehre*, for example one entitled 'Newtonische Mucken/Newton's Flies' (opposite), where he questions Newton's method of experimenting with small objects or creatures. The sum of these observations doesn't really add up to a concise 'theory' of colours so much as a detailed catalogue of their qualities.

Goethe's complete *Farbenlehre* must have been a daunting publication. Only the first, 'didactic' volume was translated into English by Charles Lock Eastlake (see pages 84–85) and it was not published until 1840. There is no doubt that *Farbenlehre* made an impression on other colour writers, academics and artists in the mid- and late nineteenth century, most notably J. W. M. Turner (see pages 82–83). Turner aside, however,

Opposite: The elaborate first plate of the third, 'historical', volume of *Farbenlehre*. It is composed of eleven separate numbered images, ranging from a simple colour wheel, to coloured shadows, the appearance of a flame against a dark background, and even to a landscape scene as it would appear to a person suffering from a particular kind of colour blindness.

direct references to Goethe's colour studies are notably rare in English literature before the 1840s. In the preface to his translation Eastlake notes the criticism Goethe's theory had received in the years immediately after its publication. He acknowledges that while some of it was justified, some was self-inflicted by Goethe, who had been unnecessarily harsh and uncompromising in his attacks on Newton's much-respected *Opticks*. However, he argues that with the passing of 30 years a calmer and less-vindictive assessment of Goethe was possible and that there was much in his observations that was very useful to a wide range of artists and thinkers, and that, likewise, Newton's theory had its shortcomings, omissions and fanciful elements. A particular merit of Goethe's work, according to Eastlake, was his applicability of colour theory to the arts and his focus on 'the phenomena of contrast and gradation, two principles which may be said to make up the artist's world, and to constitute the chief elements of beauty.'

John Gage suggested that in Germany in the 1840s, Goethe's colour theory had a low reputation among artists and was not often mentioned in related literature until much later. Nevertheless, seen in the greater context of Romantic and later art and philosophy, Goethe did have a substantial legacy in a new generation of artists and writers who began to consider subjective colour perception, emotional responses and analogies between colours and character qualities and moral connotations. One of the earliest examples of Goethe's impact was Arthur Schopenhauer's important philosophical treatise *Über das Sehn und die Farbe* (*On Vision and Colours*), published privately in 1816 following conversations between the two writers. It did not reach a wide audience, but a revised and extended edition was published in 1854. Another author influenced directly by Goethe was the German physiologist Johannes Peter Müller, who had studied *Farbenlehre* in preparation for a scientific publication on the physiology of sight in 1826. Later in the nineteenth century we see a slow but steady increase in the appreciation of his colour theory, frequently in the context of art and design and beyond the German speaking area. In 1867 an article by British decorator John Gregory Crace, of the famous Crace Firm, entitled 'On Colour', discussed at great length the concept of colour contrast and Crace noted that 'several men of high attainments have written upon this subject, more particularly Goëthe [sic], who published his interesting work "The Doctrine of Colours" in 1810, and it has since been translated by Sir Charles Eastlake, who added to it notes of great interest and usefulness.' He also references Field and Chevreul, but it is Goethe's experiments and writings he appears to rate most highly. In one instance Crace compares an observation he made of coloured shadows to Goethe's example of a dark after-image of a white girl's face. By contrast, he says about Chevreul: 'Though I highly appreciate and admire his theories, I do not always agree with him when he regulates decorative effects of colour.'

The twentieth century saw a great reappraisal and appreciation for Goethe's colour work and colour theory in general, especially among abstract and Modernist artists. Philosophers, too, continued to be inspired by *Farbenlehre*, most notably by the Austrian-British Ludwig Wittgenstein in *Bemerkungen über die Farben* (*Remarks on Colour*), written in 1950/1 but first published posthumously in 1977.

THE TEMPERAMENT ROSE

The colour wheel opposite was drawn in *c.* 1799 during an excited (and inebriated) exchange about colour between Goethe and Friedrich Schiller. Entitled *Temperamenten-Rose* (*Temperament Rose* or *Vane*), the German poets were making a visual analogy between colours and the ancient concept of the four bodily humors, resembling four basic temperaments: choleric, sanguine, melancholy and phlegmatic, and assigned specific occupations and character traits to each group. For example, according to Goethe and Schiller, teachers can be found in the phlegmatic group, while lovers and bon vivants are of a sanguine nature. Rulers are among the melancholy, but in close proximity to choleric tyrants. In an earlier sketch Goethe assigned sensual and character qualities to colours, such as 'good', 'powerful' and 'gentle'. Goethe later explored these seemingly unscientific associations and analogies in the didactic part of the 1810 edition of his *Farbenlehre*. Colour order systems based on the concept of the four temperaments have been mooted since at least classical times, but the addition of specific human character types was at first probably an experimental and playful take, resulting from the exchange with Schiller. However, the extent to which Goethe later applied moral values to colours can perhaps be attributed to his exchanges and friendship with many contemporary Romantic artists and writers, who explored the relationship between the individual and natural order in the widest sense.

Opposite: Goethe's *c.* 1799 *Temperamenten-Rose*. As Newton drew analogies between colour and music, here Goethe and Schiller relate colour to the four humours and associated character types, extrapolating further to various occupations.

Observing Newton in the Garden

Humphry Repton was an English draughtsman and designer who embarked on a career in landscape gardening in 1788, not long after the death of Lancelot 'Capability' Brown in 1783. Repton quickly established himself as the leading landscape designer in Britain and published widely on architecture, design and landscape gardening, sometimes challenging aesthetic ideas of the Picturesque; at other times, embracing them. In particular, he was interested in how the four elements of the art of painting – composition, design or drawing, expression and colouring – could be applied to his work. In an 1803 publication entitled *Observations on the Theory and Practice of Landscape Gardening*, he noted the importance of the careful application of colour to ornament: 'improper colouring may destroy the intended effect of the most correct design and render ridiculous what would otherwise be beautiful.'

Repton was particularly interested in colour both as a product of and in relation to light. In the same book, he informed the reader of his conversations with the politician William Wilberforce about a 'new theory of colours and shadows' he'd read of in an article by the mathematician Dr Isaac Milner. Milner's theory dealt with the principle of complementary colours and ideas of colour harmony as expressed by many other theorists in the early nineteenth century. What may have impressed Repton, who was particularly concerned with the effects of light on colour, was Milner's effortless explanation of Newton's experiments with immaterial colour, which he applied to light conditions in nature, with notes on how the human eye reacts and adjusts to changing light conditions. Milner also offered practical advice concerning material colour. Repton was so taken with Milner's article that he went to great lengths to obtain permission to reproduce it in full in *Observations*.

In his last publication before his death, *Fragments on the Theory and Practice of Landscape Gardening* (1816), Repton devoted an entire chapter each to the themes of contrast and colour. He elaborated on contrasts observed in a landscape in respect of light conditions and how they affect the appearance of foliage, and further discussed the colour schemes of gardens and the varieties of texture and size of plants and flowers. The chapter 'Of Colours' gives recommendations not only for the use of colour in gardens but also in landscape paintings and the colouring of prints, based on experiments with prisms that he carried out himself. Repton then provided instructions for the colourers of his own prints, based on his observations and experiments. These instructions give a rare insight into the production of books containing hand-coloured plates in the early nineteenth century:

As the Plates in my former work employed a great number of women and children in colouring them, I expect to render the process much more easy in this present work, by the following instructions given to the printer and colourer. The Plates to be printed in a bluish-grey ink (this is the neutral tint for the light and shade of the Landscape); the colourer to wash in the sky with blue or violet, &c. according to each sketch; also going over the distances with the same colour; then wash the foregrounds and middle distances with red, orange, or yellow, copying the drawings; and when dry, wash over with blue, to produce the greens in the middle distances: this being done as a dead colouring, a few touches with the hand of the master, and a harmonizing tint to soften the whole, will produce all the effect expected from a coloured print.

Repton included in this chapter a plate (opposite) that shows the colours he observed during his prism experiments, as well as a 'Diagram to explain the Harmony of Colours' in a star-shaped design, and diagrams illustrating the duality of cold and warm tints and their uses in a painting – 'for sky & distances' and 'for the foregrounds', respectively. Two pictorial images show his theories applied to a landscape early in the morning, before and just after sunrise.

While Repton was discussing colour theory predominantly still in the context of landscape gardening and landscape painting, the fact that he considered his own findings useful for producing and colouring prints is typical of the interdisciplinary nature of colour studies in the nineteenth century and is indicative of architects and designers beginning to see a practical use for colour theory in the early nineteenth century, anticipating David Ramsay Hay's *Laws of Harmonious Colouring, Adapted to House-Painting*, published just twelve years later.

Opposite: Among other details included on this plate of *Fragments* (1816), Repton gives the 'Relative Proportions' of each colour in Newton's colour wheel, where violet dominates with 80 degrees assigned it, ahead of blue and green with 60 degrees each. Repton was particularly interested in immaterial colour and how light affects the appearance of interiors and exteriors.

A   B   C

RED

Violet   Orange

Blue, or cold neutral tints

Diagram
to explain the
Harmony of Colours

Orange or warm tint

for Sky & distances

for the foregrounds

BLUE   YELLOW

Green

Morning, after the Sun is risen.   Morning twilight, before Sun rise.

Relative
Proportions
45 Red
27 Orange
48 Yellow
60 Green
60 Blue
40 Indigo
80 Violet
360 parts
according to S.^r
I.^s Newton's scale
of Quantity

London. Published by J. Taylor, Feb. 1, 1816.

Reading Colour: William Oram's Memorandums

The architect and painter William Oram wrote about the use of colour in landscape painting in the second half of the eighteenth century and planned to publish a treatise on the subject. For some unknown reason this never happened, but after his death in 1777 his widow gave his manuscripts to a certain Charles Clarke, who described himself as 'a near relative' of Oram's. Clarke edited and published the manuscript in 1810, at the beginning of a great surge in new publications on many aspects of colour and painting, perhaps seeing a financial opportunity. Oram's treatise is much concerned with composition and perspective, but he combines this with practical notes on which pigments to use and how to combine them. The final chapter is titled 'A palette of colours for painting skies and buildings', and offers simple lists and tables of colours. Oram stressed the importance of observation, meticulously describing the colours of nature in changing weather and light conditions.

The book does not differ greatly from other writings on landscape painting from the period, but the illustrations are unusual and resourceful. Clarke decided not to include coloured illustrations, possibly to keep the cost of the book down. Instead, the images have descriptions of colour printed onto the relevant areas. The editor refers to this as a colour or picture 'memorandum'. The plates are not too dissimilar to an artist's quick pencil sketches annotated with comments about colour, light and shade, but here the notes are instructive and carefully chosen. Often the notes are a shortened version of Oram's much more detailed text. A sky in his 'Memorandum of a Picture by Nicholas Poussin' (far right), for example, is described as 'light warm' in one area and 'darkish purple and soft broke with a little yellow' in an adjacent area. A hill in the foreground is 'whitish but the whole dark soft and strong enamelled much in the general look or hue'. The simpler 'Memorandum of a Sky' (right) is still fascinating in the number of colours it details as all appearing in one sky – reds, blues, greens, yellows and purples – a variety that might seem natural to the eye but which is made explicit and strange when written; and also that 'light', as well as warmth, are considered renderable qualities, as in 'Yellow greenish light all along' and 'Darkest Warm Purple'.

It is not known who created the plates, but they clearly illustrate Oram's observational, yet highly personal, accounts of colour arrangement. These memorandums inadvertently create sometimes confusing and sometimes poetic images of the colour scheme of a painting or an observed scene. You can literally read colour here.

Right: Oram's memorandum paints a technicolour sky, with 'Greenish blue light' in the top left, 'All red light' in the foreground cloud, 'Yellow greenish light all along' the middle, and 'Darkest Warm Purple' in the lowest cloud.

Opposite: The 'Memorandum of a Picture by Nicholas Poussin' gives more detail of particular features in comparison to each other, such as the 'Dark blue hills ... bluer than the sky next them'.

48 ROMANTIC IDEAS AND NEW TECHNOLOGIES – THE EARLY NINETEENTH CENTURY

Pl. 5. pa. 62.

Fine blue

Light Warm

Darkish Purple and soft broke with a little Yellow

Strong brown oker black & white much darker than the Sky

Dark blue hills made with blue white and light red, bluer than the Sky next them

Strong and dark

very Brown   Whitish

Whitish but the whole dark soft and strong enamelled much in the general look or hue

I.S. sculp.

Memorandum of a Picture by

NICHOLAS POUSSIN,

Sold by Auction 16.th Dec.r 1756.

Publish'd Aug.t 1, 1810, by White & Cochrane, Fleet Street.

Mary Gartside's Abstract Colour Blots

Opposite & overleaf: With these colour blots, Gartside's aim was to reduce examples of harmonious compositions to their colour layout and show degrees of brightness within the colours. The colours she chose to illustrate in this way roughly follow Newton's spectrum, although, like Claude Boutet, she includes two shades of red instead of two types of blue (see page 18).

Between 1805 and 1808 the little-known painter Mary Gartside published three books on painting in watercolour that reflect an interest in the practical applicability of colour theory. Little is known about Gartside's life except that she taught watercolour painting to ladies and exhibited some of her own botanical drawings at the Royal Academy in 1781 and at other London venues until 1808. While it was acceptable for women to teach watercolour painting, it was less common for them to publish so extensively in the field.

Gartside's first book, privately published and printed in London by T. Gardiner in 1805, was modestly titled *An Essay on Light and Shade, on Colours, and on Composition in General*. It was intended for Gartside's students and at first glance is nothing more than a painting manual for ladies, like its very short predecessor, a pamphlet entitled *An Essay on Light and Shadow* (c. 1804). However, a closer look at its content, style and illustrations makes it clear that this was more than an amateur's manual. An extended but otherwise quite similar second edition of the work in 1808, published by William Miller, was boldly renamed *An Essay on a New Theory of Colours*.

Like many of her contemporaries, Gartside referred directly to Isaac Newton and Moses Harris, while also showing some sympathy for Goethe's dualistic colour system. What makes Gartside's *Essay* stand out among the wealth of illustrated books on colour and painting published in her lifetime is the way she illustrated it. Apart from two standard tables of seven prismatic and compound colours (reminiscent of Harris, but in the shape of boxes) and a colour wheel, she illustrated eight tints in a most unusual manner. The tints (white, yellow, orange, green, blue, scarlet, violet and crimson) roughly follow Newton's prismatic spectrum, with the addition of white. These plates are full page, freely painted watercolour 'blots', showing the named tint at various degrees of saturation, and blending abstractly with others, usually greens and browns.

Until much later in the nineteenth century there is no other example of a colour system that is as inventive, but Gartside's work was overlooked in literature until fairly recently. In 1948 her blots were discussed in relation to Moses Harris by the scholar F. Schmid, who described them as 'very fantastic and modern, suggesting paintings by the Swiss artist Giacometti, or even a Walt Disney film'.

While the combination of beauty and usefulness of Gartside's illustrations is undeniable, the inclusion of such complex hand-coloured and freely painted plates raises questions about how they were produced, who painted them, and to what degree the author was involved in the process. Even a cautiously estimated print run of between 150 and 200 for *Essay on Light and Shade* means that, in total, between 1,650 and 2,200 plates needed to be produced. It is highly improbable that Gartside, or indeed many other authors of similar books, painted all the plates for her publications herself; it is likely she engaged her young female students in the process. Her later publisher William Miller stressed her direct involvement with image production and used this as a selling point. In an advertisement placed in the *Morning Post* on February 9, 1809, announcing the publication of her third book, *Ornamental Groups, Descriptive of Flowers, Birds, Shells, Fruit, Insects, &c., and Illustrative of a New Theory of Colouring* he informed potential purchasers that 'This beautiful work is printed on imperial drawing paper, and each number, containing six plates, mounted and coloured by and under Miss Gartside's immediate eye.' The labour-intensive production of any colour-illustrated book in the early nineteenth century is a reminder of how precious and expensive books still were in that period.

Blue. 7.

ROMANTIC IDEAS AND NEW TECHNOLOGIES – THE EARLY NINETEENTH CENTURY

ROMANTIC IDEAS AND NEW TECHNOLOGIES – THE EARLY NINETEENTH CENTURY

Popular Manuals for Amateur Painters

The ease of use, portability and affordability of watercolour paints and tools meant that working in and with colour became a popular pastime for many in the nineteenth century. This led to an increased demand for drawing and colouring lessons at all levels. Many girls and young women learned how to draw, and giving lessons in painting or writing instructive books about it was a welcome source of supplementary income for professional artists. The arrangement of colours and their relation to line drawing and tonal shading of a composition was considered highly complex, resulting in hundreds of instructive manuals being published in Britain in the first three decades of the nineteenth century.

An early example of an instructive manual to painting in watercolour is English landscape painter David Cox's *A Series of Progressive Lessons, Intended to Elucidate the Art of Landscape Painting in Water Colours* (1811). Cox acknowledged a basic order of three primaries and three secondaries in painting, and recommended a reduced palette of subtle, mixed colours, though the focus of his book is on available pigments, composition and paint mixture rather than colour theory. Cox's 'progressive method' of painting involved the gradual development of a picture from the first rough sketch to the final thing through several stages of increasingly complex and detailed colour application. In the instructions for making a picture, the text is actually interspersed with watercolour samples painted into small outlined rectangles next to the pigment names (see above right). Cox's popular manual went into nine editions until 1845, with ever-increasing quality and variety of illustration, and he published other books in a similar style.

In the 1820s the Scottish painter and engraver John Burnet published a series of artists' manuals that would go into many editions in the nineteenth century and be translated into other European languages. Like others before and after him, he drew on examples from Dutch, Flemish and Venetian masters when explaining and illustrating his methods. Having moved on from William Oram (see pages 48–49), using coloured illustrations when discussing the topic of colour was now non-negotiable. Utilising his engraving skills, Burnet provided most of the copperplate engravings, along with extensive hand-colouring, himself.

The first plate of eight in a volume dedicated entirely to colour, *Practical Hints on Colour in Painting* (1827), includes five colour diagrams, plus two figurative scenes depicting light and shade, which are coloured entirely by hand. While delivering practical advice was Burnet's main concern, by including these five small diagrams he also provides a short and useful overview of colour order, beginning with Isaac Newton's seven-hue range (red, orange, yellow, green, blue, purple and violet) roughly reflecting Newton's proportions. As in other diagrams, indigo is sacrificed, here replaced by purple. Fig. 2 shows Leonardo da Vinci's tetrachromatic system (yellow, green, blue and red) with the addition of white and black as essential colours for the painter. The next diagram shows the system proposed by the eighteenth-century German painter Anton Raphael Mengs comprising five primaries (white, yellow, red, blue and black) and five secondary mixtures (orange, green, purple, grey and brown – still with white but now excluding black). The other two diagrams show the arrangement of warm (yellow, red and brown) and cold (grey, green and blue) colours between white and black. Burnet's practical treatises on painting remained in print in various editions until the 1850s and were reissued again later in the nineteenth century, long after his death.

Above right: Aside from detailed explanations of the progressive development of a picture, Cox includes the precise colours and colour mixtures, complete with hand-coloured visual representations, in his instructions.

Opposite: The colour diagrams shown on this plate of Burnet's *Practical Hints on Colour* include Newton's spectrum; the tetrachromatic system; a system of primaries and secondaries by Mengs; warm colours and cold colours; a brightly lit scene and a scene in shadow.

ROMANTIC IDEAS AND NEW TECHNOLOGIES – THE EARLY NINETEENTH CENTURY

A Taxonomy of Colours: *Werner's Nomenclature*

A young Charles Darwin took this book with him on the HMS Beagle and used Syme's colour names and descriptions in his notebooks

Opposite: Not quite as many as 50, Werner included eight shades of grey in his *Nomenclature*. Number 10, 'Smoke Grey' can be found on the 'Breast of the Robin round the Red' and in flint. Number 12, 'Pearl Grey', meanwhile, can be found on the 'Backs of black headed and Kittiwake Gulls', the 'Back of Petals of the Purple Hepatica' and in 'Porcelain Jasper'.

Werner's Nomenclature of Colours is a good and rather curious example of the renewed interest in colour in the early nineteenth century. It is a new edition and interpretation of the 1774 nomenclature *Von den äusserlichen Kennzeichen der Fossilien (On the external characteristics of minerals)* by German geologist Abraham Gottlob Werner, published in 1814 and reprinted in 1821 in London. Its full title is *Werner's Nomenclature of Colours, With Additions, Arranged so as to Render it Highly Useful to the Arts and Sciences, Particularly Zoology, Botany, Chemistry, Mineralogy, and Morbid Anatomy. Annexed to Which Are Examples Selected From Well-known Objects in the Animal, Vegetable, and Mineral Kingdoms.* The editor of the new edition, Patrick Syme, a flower painter at the Wernerian and Horticultural Societies in Edinburgh, illustrated the book with detailed colour lists, comprising numerous shades and variations of the colours green, orange, yellow, blue, purple, red, black, white, grey and brown. The total number of colours listed and depicted in Syme's new edition is 110, an extension from Werner's original 79 tints. Syme presented them in strict chart format (see opposite and overleaf) and added short descriptions of equivalents for each particular tint in the plant world (mostly flowers), animal world (insects and birds feature heavily) and the mineral kingdom. In his choice of colour names Syme did not always refer to pigments but instead focussed on the appearance and recognisability of a colour, as the main purpose of this publication was to help with taxonomic identification and representation.

Some colour names are wonderfully evocative, such as 'Gallstone Yellow', 'Veinous' and 'Arterial Blood Red', 'Leek Green', 'Liver Brown' and 'Skimmed Milk White'. Perhaps not surprisingly, a young Charles Darwin took a copy of Syme's *Werner's Nomenclature* with him on the HMS *Beagle* voyage to South America and Australia between 1831 and 1836, and used Syme's colour names and descriptions in his notebooks. Small, handy charts like these were of use to both scientists and artists, as they could fit into a small bag and be consulted while observing nature, whether it was for the purpose of identification, accurate visual representation or artistic inspiration. Although simpler in design than complex colour wheels or similar diagrams, the breakdown of one colour into a variety of tints within that colour – for example, Syme lists eighteen types of red – with added actual examples from the natural world and individual colour swatches, was of great practical use when identifying and recording the many varieties of colours we see around us. This need for detailed colour lists was strong in Werner's and Syme's period, but the lists would grow even longer and more detailed in the nineteenth and twentieth centuries.

What makes this little book special in a purely material sense is that the colour samples are not painted onto the pages but onto separate sheets of paper, which were then cut into small squares and eventually stuck onto the pages. It is assumed that Syme enlisted the help of his family with this laborious task.

GREYS.

Nº	Names.	Colours.	ANIMAL.	VEGETABLE.	MINERAL.
9	Ash Grey.		Breast of long tailed Hen Titmouse.	Fresh Wood ashes	Flint.
10	Smoke Grey.		Breast of the Robin round the Red.		Flint.
11	French Grey.		Breast of Pied Wag tail.		
12	Pearl Grey.		Backs of black headed and Kittiwake Gulls.	Back of Petals of Purple Hepatica.	Porcelain Jasper.
13	Yellowish Grey.		Vent coverts of White Rump.	Stems of the Barberry.	Common Calcedony.
14	Bluish Grey.		Back, and tail Coverts Wood Pigeon.		Limestone
15	Greenish Grey.		Quill feathers of the Robin.	Bark of Ash Tree.	Clay Slate. Wacke.
16	Blackish Grey.		Back of Nut-hatch.	Old Stems of Hawthorn.	Flint.

GREENS.

No.	Names	Colours	ANIMAL	VEGETABLE	MINERAL
46	Celandine Green.		Phalæna Margaritaria.	Back of Tussilago Leaves.	Beryl.
47	Mountain Green.		Phalæna Viridaria.	Thick leaved Cudweed, Silver leaved Almond.	Actynolite Beryl.
48	Leek Green.			Sea Kale, Leaves of Leeks in Winter.	Actynolite Prase.
49	Blackish Green.		Elytra of Melöe Violaceus.	Dark Streaks on Leaves of Cayenne Pepper.	Serpentine.
50	Verdigris Green.		Tail of small long tailed Green Parrot.		Copper Green.
51	Bluish Green.		Egg of Thrush.	Under Disk of Wild Rose leaves.	Beryl.
52	Apple Green.		Under Side of Wings of Green Broom Moth.		Chrysoprase.
53	Emerald Green.		Beauty Spot on Wing of Teal Drake.		Emerald.

GREENS.

No.	Names	Colours	ANIMAL	VEGETABLE	MINERAL
54	Grass Green.		Scarabæus Nobilis.	General Appearance of Grass Fields. Sweet Sugar Pear.	Uran Mica.
55	Duck Green.		Neck of Mallard.	Upper Disk of Yew Leaves.	Ceylanite.
56	Sap Green.		Under Side of lower Wings of Orange tip Butterfly.	Upper Disk of Leaves of woody Night Shade.	
57	Pistachio Green.		Neck of Eider Drake.	Ripe Pound Pear. Hypnum like Saxifrage.	Cryolite.
58	Asparagus Green.		Brimstone Butterfly.	Variegated Horse-Shoe Geranium.	Beryl.
59	Olive Green.			Foliage of Lignum vitæ.	Epidote Olivine Ore.
60	Oil Green.		Animal and Shell of common Water Snail.	Nonpareil Apple from the Wall.	Beryl.
61	Siskin Green.		Siskin.	Ripe Colmar Pear. Irish Pitcher Apple.	Uran Mica.

YELLOWS.

No.	Names	Colours	ANIMAL	VEGETABLE	MINERAL
62	Sulphur Yellow.		Yellow Parts of large Dragon Fly.	Various Coloured Snap dragon.	Sulphur.
63	Primrose Yellow.		Pale Canary Bird.	Wild Primrose.	Pale coloured Sulphur.
64	Wax Yellow.		Larva of large Water Beetle.	Greenish Parts of Nonpareil Apple.	Semi Opal.
65	Lemon Yellow.		Large Wasp or Hornet.	Shrubby Goldylocks.	Yellow Orpiment.
66	Gamboge Yellow.		Wings of Goldfinch, Canary Bird.	Yellow Jasmine.	High coloured Sulphur.
67	Kings Yellow.		Head of Golden Pheasant.	Yellow Tulip, Cinque foil.	
68	Saffron Yellow.		Tail Coverts of Golden Pheasant.	Anthers of Saffron Crocus.	

YELLOWS.

No.	Names	Colours	ANIMAL	VEGETABLE	MINERAL
69	Gallstone Yellow.		Gallstones.	Marigold Apple.	
70	Honey Yellow.		Lower Parts of Neck of Bird of Paradise.		Fluor Spar.
71	Straw Yellow.		Polar Bear.	Oat Straw.	Scorlite. Calamine.
72	Wine Yellow.		Body of Silk Moth.	White Currants.	Saxon Topaz.
73	Sienna Yellow.		Vent Parts of Tail of Bird of Paradise.	Stamina of Honey-suckle.	Pale Brazilian Topaz.
74	Ochre Yellow.		Vent Coverts of Red Start.		Porcelain Jasper.
75	Cream Yellow.		Breast of Teal Drake.		Porcelain Jasper.

These pages: Some pages from the 1821 edition of Syme's *Werner's Nomenclature*, with the lists of colour samples, their names and where they could be found in flora, fauna and geology.

Among the greens is an 'Emerald Green', which can be seen on the 'Beauty Spot on Wing of Teal Drake'. One of the yellows is a 'Straw Yellow' that resembles the colour of a polar bear, while 'Vine Yellow' is supposed to look like the body of a silk moth. 'Arterial Red' is the colour of the corn poppy, and 'Veinous Blood Red' that of a musk flower, according to this list.

ROMANTIC IDEAS AND NEW TECHNOLOGIES – THE EARLY NINETEENTH CENTURY

George Field: Science, Art and Symbolism

George Field was a British colourman, pigment-maker, chemist and colour researcher. His first book on colour, *Chromatics, or, An Essay on the Analogy and Harmony of Colours*, was published in 1817 and he continued to write and publish on colour until his death, with further revised and expanded editions of his works being published until the 1880s. His steady output, commercial success, connections with the art world and his wide-ranging research interests make Field's work perhaps the best example of the nature of colour literature, and the changing attitudes towards colour and pigment use, in the nineteenth century. In style, format and presentation *Chromatics* resembles slightly earlier illustrated books on colour and colour theory, such as Mary Gartside's *Essay on Light and Shade* (1805) (see pages 50–53) and James Sowerby's *New Elucidation of Colours* (1809). Field follows in the tradition of attempting to present colour systems visually, across a wide variety of charts including pyramidal shapes, hexagons, variations on the colour circle, various trapezoidal shapes, and overlapping triangles forming stars. His colour stars (overleaf) are particularly striking. They illustrate a chapter in which Field examines the harmonious combination of colours at various stages of mixing. At the heart of each star is always a black or a very dark tint, indicative of Field illustrating colour systems concerned with subtractive colour, that is, paints and pigments, rather than additive coloured light.

Field's approach was rooted in his firm belief that the sciences and arts are intrinsically linked and 'mutually reflect light upon each other'. Like Goethe, Field argued for a basic colour principle of duality and also for symbolic, moral or psychological associations of colour, where yellow and blue form a polarity associated with light and shade, as well as with activity and passivity. In the same way that Goethe combined the concept of polarity with a symmetrical colour system based on three primaries (or primitives) and three secondaries, Field, too, recognised and promoted the concept of three primary colours. A practising Christian as well as a serious scientist, Field associated the trichromatic concept of three primary colours with Christian concepts of the Holy Trinity, going as far as to identify the purest and most stable pigments as earthly representations of this vision, namely red madders, lemon yellow and ultramarine blue.

Left: George Field's works went into many editions. This is the hand-coloured frontispiece from a 1841 edition of *Chromatography*, showing a highly developed version of a colour wheel.

Right: Pages from *Chromatics* illustrating Field's concept of primary, secondary and tertiary in practical mixing terms.

Overleaf: Field's colour stars are a particularly beautiful representation of the principles of colour mixing. The black at the heart of each star is a clear indication that we are dealing with material or subtractive colour.

62   **ROMANTIC IDEAS AND NEW TECHNOLOGIES** – THE EARLY NINETEENTH CENTURY

Experimenting with pigments and pigment manufacture from as early as 1804, Field recorded his observations in extensive notebooks and was particularly concerned with the invention of tools and machines for the extraction, filtration and production of pigments. From 1808 he began supplying pigments to artists; other colourmen including William Winsor and Henry Newton, who in 1832 founded Winsor & Newton; tradespeople; artists' suppliers; and printers and publishers, including Rudolph Ackermann. Field was responding not only to the need for high-quality pigments, but also to the need for scientifically sound and reliable information on colour and pigments. This would explain the continued popularity of Field's publications, all of which went into several expanded or revised editions. Field's pigments literally stood the test of time and were from the 1850s onwards praised by the colour researcher Mary Philadelphia Merrifield (see pages 104–105) as well as members of the Pre-Raphaelite Brotherhood, in particular William Holman Hunt and John Everett Millais.

As well as demonstrating the new ways that colour was understood in the early nineteenth century, his sheer publishing output throughout the period makes Field's work perhaps the best example of changing methods for illustrating and producing colour books in his time. The first edition of *Chromatics* from 1817 was published in a small edition of 250 copies. All seventeen copper plates in *Chromatics* are hand-coloured in watercolour and gouache, presumably by Field himself or under his close supervision. Its price of two guineas (£2.2s.0d) reflects the high quality of the illustrations. By contrast, *Chromatography*, Field's substantial main work, published in 1835 in quarto format (33 x 30 cm), has only a hand-coloured frontispiece and one further copperplate without colour. The format of subsequent editions and other publications by Field continued to decrease in size. A new edition of *Chromatography* from 1841 is noticeably smaller (23 x 15 cm) and illustrated with only a hand-coloured frontispiece. Affordability, together perhaps with an expanding market, may be the key to these developments. A shorter version of *Chromatography*, titled *Rudiments of the Painters' Art: Or, A Grammar of Colouring* (1850, 1858), published in the last years of his life, is of an even smaller size (18 x 10.5 cm) and presented like an artists' handbook. It contains one small hand-coloured frontispiece in the shape of a simplified colour star, as well as two lithographs and three chromo-lithographs, the latter illustrating the three primary colours in the shape of flowers (opposite and below). It was priced at only two shillings – a fraction of what his first book retailed at nearly 40 years earlier.

Left & right: Two of Field's plates from *Rudiments*, depicting primary colours in the form of flowers to represent certain qualities. Red (right) is presented in a formal, roselike image with its complementary, green. Seen left, the colours blue and yellow are presented together in more abstract forms. Field follows Goethe in assigning blue to shade and yellow to light.

COLOUR AND MUSIC

Field's beautiful, harmonious representations of colour, exemplified by his stars; the metaphysical connection he makes between his three primary colours and the Christian, Holy Trinity; and indeed the alternative title of his first publication all demonstrate a new focus within colour studies in the early nineteenth century. Alongside the need for effective visual colour systems, there was a desire to find analogies and symbolic associations. To this effect, Field, like Newton before him (and whom he referenced directly), argued a strong connection between colour and music. He saw, for example, a correspondence between the three primary colours and the notes C, E and G. He explored this analogy further in later publications and included a plate illustrating these ideas, combining a coloured triangular shape with musical scales (opposite). Just a few years later, the Scottish interior decorator David Ramsay Hay incorporated the analogy of music and colour into his publication *The Laws of Harmonious Colouring Adapted to Interior Decorations: With Observations on the Practice of House Painting* (1847) and included a similar illustration (above).

Newton was by no means the first to have made connections between colour and music. The Greek mathematician Pythagoras saw a correlation between the two, and it is possible that these associations go back even further. They are certainly a constant theme in colour theory and the performing arts. In 1650 the German scholar Athanasius Kircher published *Musurgia Universalis*, in which he discussed the possibility of a musical language based on combinations of musical notes and colour and, essentially, synaesthetic experiences.

Newton's first printed colour wheel from 1704 (see pages 12–13) followed the arrangement of the Dorian scale, and greatly inspired the French Jesuit monk Louis Bertrand Castel, who in 1734 constructed an ocular harpsichord that played only colour, followed later by models that could produce both colour and sound simultaneously. The colours of Castel's instruments took the form of pieces of paper or ribbons that would lift when keys were struck. Castel's most ambitious organ was exhibited in London in 1757, the year of his death. It was a huge device that played twelve octaves and had 144 keys and corresponding apertures that would open to reveal coloured squares of thin paper.

Above & opposite: Both Hay and Field associated lower musical notes with the darker shades and higher with brighter ones, placing a light yellow at the top of each scale. Field's system is complex and includes a large number of mixtures and what appears to be levels of saturation, while Hay's scale is more clearly based on the three primaries yellow, red and blue and their respective mixtures orange, purple and green.

EXAMPLE XVI.

ANALOGOUS SCALE OF SOUNDS AND COLOURS.

Chr. E

Instructive Palettes in Painters' Manuals

Opposite: The frontispiece to Fielding's *On Painting in Oil and Water Colours* (1839). The text notes how 'the tints are laid on the palette in a regular progression, beginning at the nearer end with white, and ending on the farthest part with the darker colours. The light colours, being most wanted, are placed most within reach.'

From the 1820s onwards we increasingly see images of palettes in painting manuals, to illustrate which colours should be used at what stage in the creation of a painting. There area few earlier examples of instructive rather than decorative or symbolic palettes in print culture, for example the fold-out plate in J. C. Le Blon's *Coloritto* (1756, pages 24–25) and William Hogarth's etching from *The Analysis of Beauty* (1753, pages 30–31). Advances in printmaking technology – aquatinting in the later eighteenth century and the invention of lithography in the early nineteenth century – encouraged ever more literal and elaborate ways of illustrating painting techniques and materials. However, all of the palettes depicted on these pages are lithographs or etchings with the actual blots of paint added by hand in watercolour. One wonders to what extent the pigments supposedly shown were actually used for painting them. Is that 'ultramarine' blot really ultramarine, or a cheaper blue posing as ultramarine for the sake of book illustration?

In the introduction to *On Painting in Oil and Water Colours for Landscape and Portraits (1839)*, the author, Theodore Henry Fielding, bemoans the 'very small number of practical treatises on Oil Painting', while 'works which treat on painting in watercolours have been so multiplied that none can complain of their scarcity'. His offering is a long and entirely practical book on the use of both media. Like John Burnet (see pages 54–57) he based his manual on his own observation as well as study of established artists, and he promoted the progressive method of painting, which he illustrated by ten etched plates, some of them hand-coloured.

The frontispiece (opposite) in particular stands out as an illustration that is both decorative and useful.

Two realistic palettes are depicted: the upper one with tints recommended for landscape painting, and the lower with tints for portraits. Underneath the palettes Fielding depicts suitable brushes. In the text, he notes that at the commencement of a painting, a palette would hold fewer tints – 'not more than two or three' – as large quantities of a few base colours must be mixed and placed initially. The contents of these two palettes are appropriate for a work in progress, when the artist requires a smaller quantity of paint but a greater range of tints. Fielding's palette frontispiece is visually pleasing and instructive, but his contemporary John Cawse had included printed and coloured palettes to illustrate his painting manuals several years earlier, and turned them into works of art in their own right.

Cawse's first publication, *Introduction to the Art of Painting in Oil Colours* (1822), was modestly illustrated but included coloured images of painters' palettes. A new and much extended edition from 1840 contained eleven expertly lithographed and then hand-coloured palettes (overleaf). They provide considerable detail about which tints should be used for the various stages of preparing backgrounds, painting portraits, landscapes and skies, and depicting fabrics such as satin in oil paint. Like Fielding, Cawse decided to illustrate these tints on a drawn palette in order to best indicate their ideal placement on the palette, for ease of mixing and to prevent certain tints from contaminating each other. The paints and pigments are remarkably accurate and brilliantly preserved in the copy shown here, but this is still an instance of watercolour and gouache being used to depict oil paint: one paint medium pretending to be another.

Plate I.

ROMANTIC IDEAS AND NEW TECHNOLOGIES – THE EARLY NINETEENTH CENTURY

These pages: A selection of palettes from John Cawse's *Introduction to the Art of Painting in Oil Colours* (1840).

Top Left: 'A palette for painting Skies, Clouds, &c. in Landscape painting.'

Left: 'A palette containing the principle tints used in Landscape painting.'

Top right: 'A palette for painting Scarlet or Crimson Satin.'

Right: 'The palette of colours for finishing the Portrait. Containing the tints laid as in the first, with the additional ones made from Lake, Brown pink, Ivory black, and Prussian blue.'

70   **ROMANTIC IDEAS AND NEW TECHNOLOGIES** – THE EARLY NINETEENTH CENTURY

The palette for painting Scarlet or Crimson Satin.

ART OF PAINTING. 33

SCARLET OR CRIMSON SATINS.

Light ochre, light red and white are the first tints for scarlet; the shadows are Indian red, and, in the darkest part, mixed with black.

The lights are vermilion and white for satin and velvet, and pure vermilion for cloth; the shade tint, vermilion, lake, and Indian red.

The reflects are light red and vermilion.

YELLOW SATIN.

The tints used in painting yellow satin are the same in number as those used for white satin, and the method of using them is the same; the lights are king's yellow; the first tint is light ochre, changed with a little of the pearl tint, made with the dark shade and white, which must be used and managed as the first tint in white satin. The middle tint is light and brown ochre, softened with the pearl tint; the shade tint is brown pink and brown ochre.

The reflects are light ochre, and, in the warmer parts, light red. The shadows are strengthened with brown pink and burnt umber.

The Palette of Colours for finishing the Portrait.

ART OF PAINTING. 27

The oils are, boiled, or drying oil, and poppy, or nut oil. The first, mixed with spirits of turpentine, in a proportion of one-third spirits to two-thirds drying oil, I have found, in practice, to be the best. All preparations of wax should be avoided, as wax prevents freedom of handling, and ultimately injures the picture, by its tendency to crack and separate.

Second Sitting for a Portrait.

Match the red and yellow tints to the complexion, and then the blues; proceed to the shadows, leaving them clear and not dark, as glazing will make them too much so; and remember, that the shadows in the dead colouring must be lighter than the finishing colours; for the finishing of shadows is by glazing, and they must always be painted thin, that they may have the quality of shade—transparency.

The light of the complexion should be painted with a full body of colour, because all whites have a tendency to sink into the ground they are painted on.

Third Sitting for a Portrait.

Lay a small quantity of clear poppy oil over the face of the portrait, and wipe it off with a piece

The 'Painter's Compass': Colour Wheels for Artists

Opposite, top: Charles Hayter's *Treatise* (1826) aimed to provide clear, straightforward information on colour. The plate entitled 'The Painter's Compass' positions the colour wheel as an essential guide for an artist, and packs in a great deal of information about colour.

Opposite, bottom: Unlike Hayter's 'Painter's Compass', Mérimée's colour wheel from 1830 is not annotated and comparatively simple. Yet it shows similar information in the way it is laid out, with the tints connecting and showing their mixtures.

In the wake of the reissue of Moses Harris's *The Natural System of Colours* (1811; see pages 26–29) and the new scientific theories of colour emerging in the early nineteenth century, many art professionals were inspired to publish handbooks that attempted to develop or adapt these colour systems in order to make them more useful to artists. The resulting books were beautifully illustrated and popularised colour theory. When it came to choosing a form in which to present a colour system, geometric designs dominated, usually in the form of wheels, discs and circles, with few figurative or fanciful depictions.

In 1826 Charles Hayter, an art teacher to the British royal family, published a practical application of colour theory that was clearly informed by Moses Harris. It also references Leonardo da Vinci's mid-sixteenth century tetrachromatic system, as proposed in his *Trattato della Pittura* (first published in English in 1721 under the title *A Treatise on Painting*). Hayter's *A New Practical Treatise on the Three Primitive Colours* (1826) proudly announced itself as 'a perfect system of rudimental information', stressing, as is typical of paint manuals of the time, its usefulness for painters.

The second plate of his book (opposite, top) is particularly appealing and meticulously coloured. Titled 'The Painter's Compass' it depicts three colour wheels of consecutive paint mixtures, divided into eighteen tints each, with three levels of brightness. They are accompanied by two white-to-black scales of warm (yellow, orange, red, purple and indigo) and cold (indigo, blue, green, yellow and pale yellow) colours. The visual and conceptual similarities to Harris are obvious, and he is indeed mentioned in the accompanying text. Perhaps referring to Newton, Hayter suggests 'the number of circular divisions may be considered as allusive to infinite, by imperceptible gradation between full colour and its total evaporation into light'. While the number of colours may in theory be infinite, Hayter was well aware of the practical and financial restrictions of depicting this in a small-format publication intended for general use. In a footnote he remarks that he had more ambitious plans regarding the images but held back, as this would have made the book too expensive.

A much simpler colour wheel, also hand-coloured, was published a few years later by French artist and chemist Jean-François-Léonor Mérimée in his treatise *De la peinture à l'huile* (1830). Mérimée focussed predominantly on materials and techniques of the old masters, but he also attempted to visualise colour order, harmony and contrast with his *échelle chromatique* (colour scale). Six coloured discs are arranged in a circle: the primaries red, yellow and blue depicted slightly larger than the secondaries orange, green and purple, all of them connected by narrow bands, with a greyish-black central disc denoting the mixture of all tints. The black disc at the centre of the wheel indicates subtractive or material colour, where the result of mixing the hues is black. Possibly, we might also see the position of black as being outside the range of colour, while the grading towards white of the bands connecting the colour circles suggests that a three-dimensional model of Mérimée's system might place white opposite the black disc.

CHAPTER III.

PLATE II.

THE PAINTER'S COMPASS.

The Three Primitive Colours here form the central datum of the first compass, according with Root 1. Plate I. which is the governing principle, and without which the *completion* of the compass must depend on the consequence of proceeding (as is the case in Harris's Treatise), while the "*root*," as *here* given, *determines*, and directs, the arrangement of every colour in the circle; leaving nothing to *chance* or "*conventional contrivance*," as each arises in its own and only proper station, dictated by their "*parent root*."

The number of circular divisions may be considered as allusive to *infinite*, by imperceptible gradation between full colour and its total evaporation into light; which I presume is sufficiently intimated by the systematical gradation of three * distinguishable variations of strength as to colour, as

---

* It was my first intention to illustrate my proposition by six large coloured plates, until I found that the expence would have been inconveniently high for many of those for whose particular instruction it was designed. I have therefore only *reduced the sizes* of the diagrams so as to comprehend the whole work; and that only (materially) in the Compasses, by giving three circular gradations instead of five; but I would advise the *practising student* to express the gradations from colour to light by many more circular degrees, increasing the number of radii at pleasure, and on as large a scale as possible, according to the system which I trust is clearly explained.

THE ART OF

PAINTING IN OIL,

AND IN

FRESCO:

BEING A

HISTORY OF THE VARIOUS PROCESSES AND MATERIALS EMPLOYED,

FROM ITS DISCOVERY, BY HUBERT AND JOHN VAN EYCK,

TO THE PRESENT TIME:

TRANSLATED FROM THE ORIGINAL FRENCH TREATISE OF

M. J. F. L. MÉRIMÉE,

SECRETARY TO THE ROYAL ACADEMY OF FINE ARTS, IN PARIS.

WITH

ORIGINAL OBSERVATIONS

ON THE RISE AND PROGRESS OF BRITISH ART, THE FRENCH AND ENGLISH CHROMATIC SCALES, AND THEORIES OF COLOURING,

By W. B. SARSFIELD TAYLOR,

SENIOR CURATOR OF THE LIVING MODEL ACADEMY, &c. &c.

LONDON:
WHITTAKER & Co. AVE MARIA LANE.
1839.

Rudolph Ackermann Colours Fashionable Society

In 1796, the young coach and carriage designer Rudolph Ackermann opened a shop in the Strand in London, producing and selling prints. A year later he also took over a small art school nearby, which he ran until 1806. This was the beginning of one of the most popular and long-lived art retail establishments in Georgian London: Ackermann's Repository of Arts. Here, Ackermann achieved huge success by combining his knowledge of design and print with advertising skills and an astute insight into fashionable London society. Within a few years the shop would also sell decorative objects and artists' materials. Ackermann also began producing some of these materials himself; for example, pressed watercolour cakes.

Ackermann also pioneered new techniques in colour printing and book illustration, and he became the leading publisher of colour plates in Britain in the early nineteenth century. He published books on a wide range of popular subjects such as design, fashion and travel. Most of these were illustrated with high-quality coloured aquatints, for which he employed the best engravers of the period. He was one of the earliest promoters of lithography and in 1819, shortly after having met its inventor, Alois Senefelder, in Germany, published the translation of Senfelder's autobiographical treatise on this revolutionary new printing method.

Between 1809 and 1829 Ackermann published the popular monthly magazine: *The Repository of Arts, Literature, Commerce, Manufactures, Fashions and Politics*, named after his famous shop (in 1829 it was renamed *Repository of Fashion*). It was dedicated to the fashion-conscious Prince of Wales (later King George IV) and was illustrated with mostly hand-coloured plates depicting the latest dress fashions (see above right), London buildings and their interiors, and furniture designs. The early issues included 'Allegorical Wood-Cut' plates, which included real samples of paper and textiles for use in design, printing, dressmaking, soft furnishing or upholstery, allowing the reader not just to see but also to feel the materials (opposite). The accompanying text for these plates helpfully informed the reader of where to purchase them. Ackermann's costume plates, fabric samples and their descriptions provide a vivid image of fashionable colours and designs, and commerce in Georgian England.

Ackermann was an astute businessman and entrepreneur who tapped into an emerging shopping culture. Shops, including his own, are frequently depicted in the magazine and shown as elegant social spaces. In the very first issue, readers were treated to a detailed interior view of Ackermann's Repository of Arts, then in 101 Strand (overleaf). Fashionably dressed men and women peruse print racks and paintings displayed on walls. Signs below the skylight advertise what can be purchased here, including 'Embossed White and Gold Ornaments' and 'Colours and Requisites for Drawing'. Behind a large serving counter are glass-fronted cabinets containing many small boxes. This is quite probably where the paints, pigments, papers and artists' tools were stored.

The business moved within the Strand a number of times and Ackermann also opened outlets in South America in the 1820s. His sons continued the Strand shop under the name Ackermann & Co. until 1861. A plate from one of the last issues of *The Repository of Arts* shows the elegant exterior of the new and enlarged premises in 96 Strand in 1827, with well-to-do Londoners flocking to it. The text informs the reader that 'It was to be expected that a place so peculiarly devoted to the arts, should, in outward appearance and internal arrangement, correspond with the nature of its establishment.'

Above right & opposite: Ackermann's Repository of the Arts magazine included hand-coloured plates depicting the latest fashions (above right), as well as woodcut plates with stuck-in samples of real fabrics (opposite).

Overleaf: Not above self-promotion, the magazine also featured images of his London shop, where it was presented it as an attractive and fashionable space.

ROMANTIC IDEAS AND NEW TECHNOLOGIES – THE EARLY NINETEENTH CENTURY

ROMANTIC IDEAS AND NEW TECHNOLOGIES – THE EARLY NINETEENTH CENTURY

ROMANTIC IDEAS AND NEW TECHNOLOGIES – THE EARLY NINETEENTH CENTURY

Frank Howard Breaks Down the Masters

Opposite, top: 'Rubens' Principle'. In this plate, the lithographic layers of blue and brown are clearly visible under the added watercolour and gouache.

Opposite, bottom: 'Ludovico Caracci's Principle'. This Venetian example is described as omitting white and black altogether, having no shades darker than a rich brown or brighter than a creamy yellow.

Himself the son of a painter, Frank Howard studied at the Royal Academy and later became an assistant to one of the most famous portrait painters of his time, Sir Thomas Lawrence. He pooled his experiences into writing artists' manuals in the smaller octavo format that was beginning to replace the quarto-format publications of the earlier nineteenth century. His manuals were mainly aimed at amateur artists but marketed as containing first-hand information from Royal Academy circles. Howard's first book on art, *The Sketcher's Manual*; or, *The Whole Art of Picture Making Reduced to the Simplest Principles*, published in 1938, deals with perspective, the pictorial arrangement of a picture, and the use of light and shadow in a drawing, but doesn't mention colour until the very last page, where he explains its omission in this book: 'Colour is reserved for a future work; both on account of its requiring more proficiency in the amateur, and on account of the extent of illustration necessary to do justice to the subject.'

The following year a volume on colour was indeed published in the same style and format, although by a different publisher. *Colour as a Means of Art: Being an Adaptation of the Experience of Professors to the Practice of Amateurs* is an important example of a painters' manual illustrated with small but high-quality colour lithographs, when lithography was still in its infancy but quickly replacing the costlier technique of aquatinting. The plates in the copy of Howard's *Colour as a Means of Art* shown here and overleaf have additions in watercolour, body colour, pencil and ink, making some of them appear almost like original paintings. We do not know who embellished the lithographs, but the hand-colouring varies greatly in each copy.

In this book, Howard provides examples of paintings by old and contemporary masters particularly noted for their use of colour, such as Titian, Rubens and Turner, and provides short chapters on their styles and 'principles'. The eighteen accompanying plates are not reproductions of works by these artists, but show images reduced to their chromatic layout. Almost all recognisable detail is omitted, giving the images an abstract quality. A similar idea was employed by several other authors of paint manuals before and after Howard, but usually in the context of describing the various stages of creating a painting (that is, the progressive method) and not for the sole purpose of illustrating colour use and layout. Howard's images stand out because they deconstruct completed oil paintings, as if we are looking at a well-known painting through a haze or with myopic eyes. From these master examples, he explains, can be derived 'certain abstract principles, which may be made the foundation for other and different arrangements, as the taste or talent of the artist or amateur may dictate. Pictures may be made up of a balance, or harmonic arrangement of Tones ... or of Colours'. These 'abstract principles' are not dissimilar to Mary Gartside's colour blots from 1805 (see pages 50–53), in which she proposed harmonious colour layouts for painting flowers in watercolour.

ROMANTIC IDEAS AND NEW TECHNOLOGIES – THE EARLY NINETEENTH CENTURY 79

Above: 'Another Principle of Titian's'. Howard describes Titian's principle as 'pure greys interspersed among masses of bright crimson, opposed to some pure white and blue, broken by flesh tints'.

Above: 'Modern Manner'. This example is clearly in the style of Turner, with emphasis on the 'white cloud which is graduated with purply greys' relieving upright and darker objects of the composition.

ROMANTIC IDEAS AND NEW TECHNOLOGIES – THE EARLY NINETEENTH CENTURY

Colour, Light and Shade: Turner's *Deluge* paintings

Above: Turner's *Shade and Darkness – the Evening of the Deluge, c.* 1843.

In or just before 1843, Joseph Mallord William Turner painted two canvasses in which he explored aspects of light and shade and the spiritual dimensions of colour in painting. Turner paired the biblical narrative themes of Noah's covenant and of Moses writing the book of Genesis with contemporary discourses on colour theory, in particular Goethe's *Zur Farbenlehre*. In fact he references Goethe directly in one of the titles: *Light and Colour (Goethe's Theory): The Morning after the Deluge, Moses Writing the Book of Genesis*. The corresponding canvas was called *Shade and Darkness – the Evening of the Deluge*.

Shade and Darkness (above) has sometimes been interpreted as a criticism of Goethe's writing, since it appears to negate light; however, one of Goethe's key arguments was that colour is created not from light, but where light and darkness meet. Where the light emanating from the centre of the canvas meets the deluge the colours are all cool blues and browns. *Light and Colour (Goethe's Theory)* (opposite), in contrast, visualises of the warm and light side of the spectrum, where the colours are predominantly red and yellow, showing a swirling and glistening splendour of light typical of Turner in his late phase. It is highly likely

Above: Turner's *Light and Colour (Goethe's Theory): The Morning after the Deluge, Moses Writing the Book of Genesis*, c. 1843.

that Turner was contemplating this argument when creating his dualistic pair of canvasses.

There is evidence that Turner participated in the intellectual discourse on colour from at least the early 1800s and read widely on the subject. He owned copies of the new edition of Moses Harris's *Natural System of Colours*, George Field's *Chromatography*, Charles Hayter's *Introduction to Perspective, Drawing and Painting* and many other publications on colour and colour theory. Some of these books contain notes in Turner's hand on the margins, including, crucially, his friend Charles Lock Eastlake's translation of the first volume of Goethe's *Farbenlehre* (overleaf), providing vital information on Turner's immersion in the subject matter. Eastlake's translation was published in 1840 as *Theory of Colours*, but it is thought he had finished it by 1820, and aspects of Goethe's colour studies were discussed in academic circles soon after its publication in German.

Art historian John Gage studied Turner's marginalia in *Theory of Colours* and came to the conclusion that Turner thought Goethe's concept of complementary colours for harmonious compositions was 'far too rigid a framework within which to understand and express the diversity of natural coloration'. Gage warned, too, that the presence of the notes as such does 'not [...] represent the painter's endorsement of Goethe's ideas of colour'.

From the evidence of his engagement with the subject, there is little doubt that over time Turner began developing his own distinct ideas about colour, colour order and use of colour appropriate to its expressive qualities. It seems likely that he was inspired by aspects of Goethe's theory while rejecting others, and these paintings are ultimately a better testament to Turner's own ideas about colour than they are an homage to Goethe.

84 **ROMANTIC IDEAS AND NEW TECHNOLOGIES** – THE EARLY NINETEENTH CENTURY

COLOURED OBJECTS DISPLACED BY REFRACTION. 107

260.

If we displace a coloured object by refraction, there appears, as in the case of colourless objects and according to the same laws, an accessory image. This accessory image retains, as far as colour is concerned, its usual nature, and acts on one side as a blue and blue-red, on the opposite side as a yellow and yellow-red. Hence the apparent colour of the edge and border will be either homogeneous with the real colour of the object, or not so. In the first case the apparent image identifies itself with the real one, and appears to increase it, while, in the second case, the real image may be vitiated, rendered indistinct, and reduced in size by the apparent image. We proceed to review the cases in which these effects are most strikingly exhibited.

261.

If we take a coloured drawing enlarged from the plate, which illustrates this experiment,* and examine the red and blue squares placed next each other on a black ground, through the prism as usual, we shall find that as both colours are lighter than the ground, similarly coloured edges and borders will appear above and below,

---

* Plate 3, fig. 1. The author always recommends making the experiments on an increased scale, in order to see the prismatic effects distinctly.

Left: Charles Lock Eastlake's translation of Goethe's *Farbenlehre*, *Theory of Colours*, was one of the books on colour that Turner consulted. While Turner approves of Goethe's concept of polarities, his notes are peppered with short, critical and challenging comments, such as 'what advance', 'prove it', 'this is doubtful' and many simple 'nos'.

Industrialism to Impressionism: The Later Nineteenth Century

Left: The beautiful dot formations from William Benson's *Principles of the Science of Colour* look like works of art in their own right, reminiscent of Damien Hirst's spot paintings, but they are in fact designed to illustrate the positions of the various colours on Benson's ambitious colour cube. This is a photograph of a page from the original 1868 book (see pages 118–119), so the warping effect here is due to the impossibility of completely flattening the pages.'

The latter half of the nineteenth century was a time of unprecedented technological advances and inventions that affected every aspect of life. The speed with which production methods, transport, fashion and ideologies were changing was breathtaking. Steam power, chemical processing, and eventually electricity changed the way people lived, worked and how things were produced. Cities expanded dramatically and quickly, while the manufacturing of goods was taking place on an ever-increasing scale as machine-production in factories continued to replace hand-production in smaller businesses. The Industrial Revolution, which had begun in the second half of the eighteenth century, reached an exciting, if sometimes threatening, peak.

The shift towards large-scale manufactured production also affected the worlds of colour, art and print culture. On a material level new technologies meant that pigments could be produced in greater quantities, and the paint and dyes created from these pigments were applied using new, industrial methods. In 1851 many of these new inventions could be seen at the Great Exhibition of the Works of Industry of All Nations in the Crystal Palace in London. In many ways, the Great Exhibition was a showcase for the new age of mass production, consumerism and industry; and use and understanding of colour were intrinsically linked to these developments. The great colourman George Field (see pages 60–67) gracefully declined to be involved on the grounds of advanced age, but a couple of his followers, the colour researcher Mary Philadelphia Merrifield and the architect and designer Owen Jones, were invited to take part and contributed to the Great Exhibition.

In book publishing, illustrators were moving away from hand-coloured metal-plate engravings towards lithography and multicoloured woodblock printing, although hand-colouring continued to be employed when maximum accuracy and precision were desired, which was frequently the case with colour diagrams and charts. The mechanical production of colour illustrations arguably led to a high degree of diversification and fragmentation in writings and publications on colour, but this was not necessarily a negative development: while we see far fewer examples of individually painted colour diagrams, many books were produced in much higher print runs than a generation or two before and therefore became affordable to a much wider readership. Among them were some of the most striking examples of colour literature ever published, such as the brilliantly executed lithographic plates by Day & Son in Owen Jones's *The Grammar of Ornament* from 1856, or

Books were produced in higher print runs and became affordable to a much wider readership

the 1850s and '60s editions of Chevreul's atlas of colour circles, with engraver and printer René-Henri Digeon's spectacular plates, produced using a four-colour aquatint printing process.

In the later nineteenth century, thinkers realised that colours can mix and influence each other optically as well as physically

Opposite: Claude Monet is best known for his endless variations on the theme of water lilies or haystacks, beautifully depicting their appearance at different times of day and in different light conditions. With its vivid hues and free brushstrokes, this painting from *c.* 1874, *Femme assise sur un Banc (Woman seated on a Bench)* (detail) is typical of the Impressionist style.

In 1841 the American artist John Goffe Rand invented collapsible metal tubes for oil paints. The patent for the UK was quickly acquired by Winsor & Newton, who added the screw top to Rand's design, and other European companies. This may sound like a minor improvement, but being able to take a selection of paints with you without having to worry about first preparing them and transferring them to small bags made of pigs' bladders, instead simply squeezing moist colour from a tube, had a profound effect on how and where painters worked.

The biggest impact of this development was felt in France when, from the 1860s to the close of the century, Claude Monet, Edgar Degas, Auguste Renoir, Camille Pissarro and a few other artists took their canvasses outdoors and made light their subject. This was the birth of Impressionism. Working *en plein air*, the artists worked quickly, as was necessary to capture the fleeting effects of the sunlight. The resulting canvasses were strangely rough in appearance, leading early critics to rubbish the new art movement. Indeed, the term 'Impressionist' was first used as an insult, delivered by critic Louis Leroy after the group's 1874 Paris exhibition, implying that the artists offered only a sketch of a scene, rather than the full and developed artworks they were expecting. The characteristic rapid brushstrokes in dabs of pure hues that give the Impressionist paintings their 'unfinished' look was, however, integral to the artists' aims.

The artists were responding to their situation, accurately translating in paint what they observed with their eye, and benefitting from the new, artificial and ready mixed colours that were ever more available as the century progressed. The extent to which they were also directly responding to the colour theories of the time has been contested, but it is certain that the work of the Impressionists aligns with the prevailing ideas about colour of the time. In earlier centuries, writers on colour typically focussed on either material or immaterial colour, frequently seeming to muddle the two, as though the different and contrary aspects of material/immaterial colour were a circle they were trying to square, and they couldn't quite make sense of how they should or could work together. In the later nineteenth century, however, we begin to see a fusion as thinkers realised that colours can mix and influence each other optically as well as physically. The optical effects of colour became the predominant concerns for thinkers like Michel Eugène Chevreul and Ogden Rood, and the Impressionists too were experimenting with the application of colour towards producing convincing representations of light.

Colour was beginning to truly infiltrate art – and it was only the beginning.

Into Darkness: M. E. Chevreul's Beautiful Science

The French chemist Michel Eugène Chevreul was the most important and influential European colour theorist of the later nineteenth century and his publications on colour contain some of the most ambitious and beautiful illustrations of the period. In the early nineteenth century he had been the assistant of Louis Nicolas Vauquelin, the Professor of Chemistry at the Museum of Natural History in Paris, who had invented a number of new pigments and dyes, including Chrome Yellow. He later succeeded Vauquelin in his role as Professor of Chemistry. In the 1820s Chevreul was employed by the Gobelin tapestry factories to investigate the quality of dye materials and problems concerning the lack of brilliance in the colour schemes of the woven tapestries. Chevreul realised that it wasn't the quality of the dyestuffs that had resulted in a dullness of the appearance of some designs, but the way in which coloured strands of wool were combined and placed close to each other. It was here that he formulated his 'laws of simultaneous contrast' that would influence and inspire designers, artists, scientist, architects and manufacturers as no other theory since Newton's had done before. Unlike most other colour researchers, he was concentrating on how

Above: One of the many impressive colour plates from the *Atlas* that accompanied Chevreul's *De la loi du contraste simultané des coleurs* from 1839. This diagram shows the effect that neutral tones – the backgrounds and the grey and black dots – have on the appearance of the colours.

90   INDUSTRIALISM TO IMPRESSIONISM – THE LATER NINETEENTH CENTURY

colours were perceived by humans, rather than their material aspects: 'In the case where the eye sees at the same time two contiguous colours, they will appear as dissimilar as possible.'

In 1828, a lecture at the Academy of Science in Paris on how colours enhance or diminish each other depending on how they are combined brought Chevreul renown throughout Europe. He finally published his findings in his main work, *De la loi du contraste simultané des couleurs* (*The laws of simultaneous contrast of colour*) in 1839. Within a year it was translated into German, and an English edition was published in 1854 under the title *The Principles of Harmony and Contrast of Colours, and Their Applications to the Arts: Including Painting, Interior Decoration, Tapestries, Carpets, Mosaics, Coloured Glazing, Paper-staining, Calico-printing, Letterpress Printing, Map-colouring, Dress, Landscape and Flower Gardening, Etc*. The lengthy title of Chevreul's book in its English edition makes it clear that his main aim was always to make colour theory applicable to a wide range of disciplines and areas of creative use of colour. The usefulness of his work is one of the main reasons for his success.

The first edition of *De la loi du contraste simultané des couleurs* comprised an impressive 735 pages of text, making it the most comprehensive treatise on colour since Goethe's *Farbenlehre*. It was accompanied by an *Atlas* of illustrations with around 40 plates, many of them coloured and some folding out to three times the width of the atlas, like the one above, depicting an 'assortment of the simple and binary colours of artists with white, black and grey'. They include relatively simple lithographed plates showing contrasts of light and dark and a number of coloured circles of hues influencing each other when placed together. Chevreul introduces an uncoloured 72-part chromatic circle (overleaf), based on the subtractive trichromatic system of yellow, blue and red as primaries. This has a flap added along its radius, which can be lifted to indicate the amount of black in each tint, a ten-part achromatic greyscale. It was an effective

Above & opposite:
Some of the plates from the 1839 *Atlas*, including Chevreul's 72-tone colour wheel with a pop-up flap, the first plate showing rectangles of light and dark greys, a seemingly random elliptical arrangement of flowers to illustrate colour harmony, and one of two plates illustrating basic colour interaction.

effective way of creating a three-dimensional colour model in two-dimensional print format.

On other plates Chevreul shows hundreds of colours in the shape of small discs, grouped to illustrate colour contrasts and harmonies. These are shown against different coloured backgrounds and painted by hand, on heavily inked lithographed plates. The 1839 *Atlas* is a most meticulous and experimental exploration of Chevreul's laws of colour contrast, expressed in the still relatively young print medium of lithography, combined with hand-colouring.

INDUSTRIALISM TO IMPRESSIONISM – THE LATER NINETEENTH CENTURY

Above: One of the huge fold-out plates from Chevreul's 1861 *Atlas*, the 'spectre solaire' presents the visible spectrum. A disclaimer at the top right corner of the plate notes that Chevreul can vouch for the accuracy of only fifteen of the colours, those marked with dotted lines down to the base.

RS

SOLAIRE

Sulfure de Carbone

M. E. CHEVREUL ne peut répondre que de l'exactitude de 15 couleurs, à savoir : Le rouge, le 5ᵉ rouge, le 4ᵉ rouge-orangé, le 5ᵉ orangé, le jaune, le 4ᵉ jaune, le jaune-vert, le 3ᵉ jaune-vert, le vert, le 3ᵉ vert, le 3ᵉ vert-bleu, le bleu, le 2ᵉ bleu, le 5ᵉ bleu et le bleu-violet — Ces couleurs sont distinguées des autres par des points...

Exécuté par les procédés Chromographiques de Digeon, brev.ᵗᵉ de S. M. l'Impératrice. Médaille de 1ʳᵉ Classe à l'Exposition
Médaille d'Argent à la Société Libre des Beaux Arts

THE ATLAS

Visually and technically, a later and larger edition of an atlas illustrating Chevreul's writings on colour is one of the most sophisticated and impressive publications on colour ever printed. In 1855 Chevreul began working with the gifted engraver René-Henri Digeon, who created colour wheels and other colour plates for Chevreul, using the 1839 chromatic circle as a guideline. They published a large volume set of colour plates together, the *Cercles Chromatiques de M. E. Chevreul*. In 1861 the *Atlas* was published again as *Exposé d'un moyen de définir et de nommer les couleurs (Proposal for a way of defining and naming colours)*, as an addition to the 33rd volume of the *Mémoires de l'Académie royale des Sciences, Paris*, and once again on its own in 1864, under the title *Des couleurs et de leurs applications aux arts industriels à l'aide des cercles chromatiques (On colours and their applications to the industrial arts with the aid of chromatic circles)*.

In the 1861 edition, shown here, the large-format *Atlas* contains twelve graded colour circles, engraved and printed in colour by Digeon (see overleaf). A preceding vertical fold-out plate, *Couleurs d'un Spectre Solaire* (see pages 94–95), displays the full prismatic spectrum of visible colours on a linear diagram against a dark background and can be used as a standard or reference for the hues found on the circles. Another plate with three columns of blue, *Gamme chromatique bleu*, acts as an example of the gradation according to the amount of white and black in it. In the 1864 edition of the *Atlas*, many more *gammes de couleurs* were included. But the most important element of the *Atlas* is Digeon's group of magnificent full-page colour circles. The first two show the pure colours at their brightest stage, one with and the one without the division into 72 sections that is included in the other circles. The following ten circles show the development from this state of maximum brightness to almost complete darkness, with an increasing addition of black to the tints. They offer a detailed visualisation of that first pop-up colour wheel from the 1839 edition. The last few circles show astonishingly subtle shades of grey and black, with just a suggestion of colour in each of them. The total number of tints in these colour wheels is 14,420, which makes these plates masterpieces of colour-printing in the later nineteenth century.

Opposite & overleaf: The twelve graded colour circles created by Chevreul. The incredible fold-out plate on the previous page is intended to illustrate the full spectrum of colours that are broken down in more detail in the following diagrams.

INDUSTRIALISM TO IMPRESSIONISM – THE LATER NINETEENTH CENTURY

INDUSTRIALISM TO IMPRESSIONISM – THE LATER NINETEENTH CENTURY

INDUSTRIALISM TO IMPRESSIONISM – THE LATER NINETEENTH CENTURY

From Science into Art: Chevreul and the Birth of Impressionism

Chevreul's work had a profound influence on many painters in the later nineteenth century, especially among the Impressionists and Post-Impressionists, who compared the use of strands of dyed wool to the application of brush strokes on a canvas. The French artist Georges Seurat was particularly interested in how colours blend optically. He studied Chevreul and other colour theories carefully, even copying out passages from their texts, and adopted their ideas into his practice by placing small strokes or dots of largely pure pigments next to each other in sometimes very large compositions. The method is often called Pointillism or Divisionism, but Seurat himself preferred the term 'chromo-luminarism'.

His paintings and his surviving palettes are a reflection of Seurat's interest in optics. Nearly all of his paintings are concerned with the changing appearance of light and colour in landscapes with figures. At least one of the many studies for his famous *Bathers at Asnières* includes a rainbow, possibly in reference to Newton, or perhaps more generally to optical studies and how they translate into painting. Seurat's working palettes seem to reflect his methodical approach to colour arrangement. On at least one of his palettes the paints are arranged in an orderly fashion along the upper edge of the square palette, in a range from dark greens and blues via reds to yellows. Each colour has been mixed carefully with white, descending halfway down the palette in brightness. A small blot of white lead paint is placed like a marker for brightness in a neat line under every colour, similar to many of his remarkably geometrical compositions, such as the one depicted here.

This painting by Seurat entitled *Seascape (Gravelines)* from 1890 clearly shows that the artist experimented with the optical blending of pure colour by means of placing distinguishable blots next to each other. Here Seurat even includes the frame in his composition and, as is typical of the Impressionist style, avoids the use of black entirely. Shades and darker areas, of which there very few, are created by colour alone, with the main focus being on the depiction of light.

Opposite: Seurat's 1890 painting, *Seascape*, transposes Chevreul's dots into a landscape painting that draws strongly on the optical colour ideas explored in Chevreul's oeuvre.

INDUSTRIALISM TO IMPRESSIONISM – THE LATER NINETEENTH CENTURY   101

A Poet's Philosophical Colour Categories

Opposite: The huge fold-out plate at the back of *La palette théorique* (1849) recognises yellow, red and blue as primary colours, and orange, purple and green as secondaries. Much of the plate is concerned with the 'nuances' – the effects of mixing beyond these first orders.

Ten years after Michel Eugène Chevreul's groundbreaking work on colour contrast *De la loi du contraste simultané des couleurs*, in 1849 another Frenchman, the relatively unknown J. C. M. Sol, published a short (61 pages) treatise on how optical theory could be applied to painting. The resulting *La palette théorique: ou, Classification des couleurs (The theoretical palette: or, Classification of colours)* was never translated from French into any other language and in academic circles it has been described as an incomplete colour system, but it is a good example of Chevreul's influence on colour literature. Sol's approach is both logical and subjective. In his various categorisations of colour he applies characteristics such as 'sad' and 'attractive' to colours, as well as ordering them in accordance with Immanuel Kant's 'table of judgements' – the concept of how we think about and understand objects according to categories such as 'quality', 'relation' and 'modality', as first formulated in 1781 in *Kritik der reinen Vernunft (Critique of Pure Reason)*.

This integration of diverse concepts into colour theory is highly reminiscent of Johann Wolfgang von Goethe's approach (see pages 42–45). Sol is known to have tried (and failed) to obtain a copy of Goethe's *Farbenlehre* and it is obvious that he was following the critical discussions concerning the German poet's colour theory. Like Goethe, Sol is critical of Isaac Newton and, incidentally, he also published poetry.

His short treatise, derivative and incomplete as it may be, stands out with regard to an unusually large plate that illustrates his proposed colour categories. In the style of maps often found in many eighteenth- and nineteenth-century publications, the plate is tipped in at the back of the book and unfolds to a sheet measuring 46.5 x 65 cm, more than double the size of the book's print block. The lithographed plate contains linear tables, charts and a starburst diagram, with tints depicted as small discs, coloured by hand. Sol's idea was perhaps similar to Newton's more than 130 years earlier: that the reader could consult the fold-out sheet while reading the main body of the text. The example shown here is inscribed and signed by Sol in the top right corner.

LA PALETTE THÉORIQUE
ou
CLASSIFICATION DES COULEURS.
par J.-C.-M SOL.

Comme un gage de l'amitié de l'auteur à Mr. Victor Guilmer.

Tableau Synthétique

1re Catégorie	2ème Catégorie			3ème Catégorie				
Sphérul principe vierge	Couleurs connexitives			Teintes Hybrides				
	Primaires	Binaires	Ternaire	Les primaires et le blanc combinés	Les binaires et le blanc combinés	Le ternaire et le blanc combiné	Les nuances d'ordre ternaire et le blanc combinés	
1re Colonne	2ème Colonne	3ème Colonne	4e Colonne	5e Colonne	6e Colonne	7e Colonne	8e Colonne	9e Colonne

2e Catégorie. Nuances d'ordre ternaire.

2e Catégorie
Nuances d'ordre binaire.

3e Catégorie
Nuances d'ordre hybride.
(trois exemples.)

I Binaire initiateur
NN Nuances
TT Ternaire évolution de la nuance

A Woman Travels in Search of Colour

Opposite: Regrettably, Merrifield's works on colour and painting techniques are only sparsely illustrated with a few line engravings or monochromatic lithographs – as was usual for small handbooks on painting practice. However, the engraving and decorated initial letter adorning the beginning of her essay for the 1851 Great Exhibition are delightful takes on the common motifs of painters' palettes and rainbows, representing colour as a source of inspiration and creativity.

Until well into the twentieth century, few women published works on colour; Mary Gartside was one of them (see pages 50–53). Born around the time Gartside was first publishing, Mary Philadelphia Merrifield left a significant mark on colour research and literature in the nineteenth century. It is not known how Merrifield acquired her education at a time when it was not possible for women to attend university, but, like Gartside, she must have moved in sufficiently privileged circles to receive a solid home education and be able to pursue self-directed study at her leisure. There are some examples of women participating in scientific research in the eighteenth and nineteenth centuries, but it is notable that their methods tend to be observational rather than experimental, and frequently, as we have seen in Gartside's case, their publications took the form of artistic manuals for other middle- or upper-class ladies, rather than serious scientific treatises. Merrifield's work falls partly into the latter category, although she obviously enjoyed not only financial freedom but also an unusual level of support, both morally and practically, from her husband and children. Merrifield is best known for the first English translation of Cennino Cennini's *Libro dell'arte* (*A Treatise on Painting, Written by Cennino Cennini in the Year 1437*), published in 1844. In it she refers to the famous colourman George Field, and praises the high quality and permanence of his pigments. Following the success of her translation, Merrifield was promptly commissioned by Prime Minister Robert Peel's government to travel to France and Italy in order to identify and transcribe medieval and Renaissance manuscripts on colour, and research the make-up of early pigments and Italian methods of painting. The trip resulted in several important publications, including *Original Treatises, Dating from the XIIth to XVIIIth Centuries on the Arts of Painting* (1849).

Although Merrifield is best known for translating historical colour literature, she also wrote about the colour theory as applied to art and architecture, for example a critical essay about Owen Jones's colour scheme for the interior of Joseph Paxton's Crystal Palace, site of the Great Exhibition of Industry of All Nations, in 1851. The essay was titled 'The Harmony of Colours as Exemplified in the Exhibition', suggesting that Merrifield was responding to ideas about colour and colour arrangement developed a generation earlier. In the essay she not only explains Jones's scheme but also touches on ways in which shapes and objects in interior design influence the use of colour and choice of pigments. She concluded that the same principles apply to painting a picture and designing an interior or decorative objects:

The attainment of a good and harmonious style of colour in painting is the result of much observation and study, not only of nature, but of the works of other artists: the same steps must be followed in Art-manufactures, or the same results will not be attained. When the principles by which the harmony of colour is regulated are clearly understood, they are easily carried into practice.

From the early 1850s, Merrifield also authored several guidebooks giving practical advice on painting and drawing in a series published by Winsor & Newton, including one titled *Light and Shade* – perhaps in reference to Gartside's first publication on colour. In these books she condensed her remarkable knowledge of many aspects of colour, gained largely through self-directed study and observation. These books went into many editions and were still being reissued by Winsor & Newton after her death. In fact, some of them are still in print now. Like the posthumous shorter and smaller editions of George Field's works on colour, they are typical examples of concise and affordable handbooks on art that began to appear in the mid-nineteenth century and appealed to a large readership.

104   INDUSTRIALISM TO IMPRESSIONISM – THE LATER NINETEENTH CENTURY

The Harmony of Colours as exemplified in the Exhibition

By Mrs. MERRIFIELD.

George Barnard Cuts Up Pages

George Barnard was a British drawing teacher whose intention was to provide a comprehensive and richly illustrated guidebook about the art of painting landscapes in watercolour for amateur artists as well as students of art. His substantial *The Theory and Practice of Landscape Painting in Water-Colours* was first published in 1855 and contains 69 small woodcuts and 30 high-quality coloured lithographs using the Leighton Brothers' 'Chromatic Process'. George Cargill Leighton had been trained by the printer George Baxter and greatly improved Baxter's highly successful method of multicoloured printing combining a variety of inks, colours and printing plates.

Many of the images in the book illustrate the different stages of picture composition and execution, but there are also several plates on the basics of colour theory. One, for example, shows the prismatic range against a dark background and another one visualises the principle of primary, secondary and tertiary colours by means of overlaid strips of colour (see overleaf). As this plate suggests, Barnard's s colour system is firmly material – relating colour always to the mixing of pigments. The colour diagrams he included are relatively simple in design but printed with heavily inked plates, which gives them a marked solidity and glossiness.

In the diagram on the opposite page, Barnard has arranged 'twenty-five of the most useful pigments' in a diamond formation. The diagram was designed as a more schematic alternative to the paintbox depicted in a woodcut on the book's preceding page (above), having 'an order approximating to that which [the pigments] occupy in the box, and at the same time extended in such a manner as to present to the eye, at one view, an harmonious arrangement of colours'. Greens are noticeably absent in the diagram. Although essential in the genre of landscape painting, they would have been mixed from high-quality yellows and blues like those included at the top and bottom of the diagram.

It is significant that Barnard places this image not in the opening chapter on 'The Nature of Colour' but in the second, on 'Materials', stressing the applicability of colour theory to the painter's art. Order and a systematic approach to tools are advocated by Barnard: 'The pigments should always occupy the same position in relation to each other, in order that there may be no hesitation in dipping the brush into the colour required.'

Barnard dedicated the second edition of his book (from 1858, pictured on these pages) to the great scientist Michael Faraday, who had discovered the effects of magnetism on light and created the first

Above & opposite: The diamond-shaped diagram seen opposite is a graphic representation of a paintbox ordered harmoniously, as seen in the woodcut illustration seen above.

HARMONIOUS ARRANGEMENT
OF TWENTY-FIVE OF THE MOST USEFUL PIGMENTS.

1. LEMON YELLOW.
2. GAMBOGE.
3. INDIAN YELLOW.
4. CADMIUM.
5. YELLOW OCHRE.
6. RAW SIENNA.
7. ORANGE CHROME.
8. MARS ORANGE.
9. BURNT SIENNA.
10. LIGHT RED.
11. VERMILION.
12. ROSE MADDER.
13. CRIMSON LAKE.
14. VENETIAN RED.
15. INDIAN RED.
16. PURPLE MADDER.
17. BROWN MADDER.
18. VAN. BROWN.
19. BROWN PINK.
20. SEPIA.
21. PAYNE'S GRAY.
22. IVORY BLACK.
23. INDIGO.
24. FRENCH BLUE.
25. COBALT.

LEIGHTON, BROTHERS.

PLATE 4.

Above: Simple overlaid translucent strips neatly demonstrate the principles mixing primary colours and secondaries.

Opposite: Reminiscent of Mary Gartside's colour blots, Barnard includes a plate showing the effects of combinations of colours on each other.

Overleaf: A plate faced with a blank page, cut horizontally in half, allows the reader to view one part of the plate at a time, or both at once, in order to better compare the effects of the contrasts that the plate depicts.

electric current, thus paving the way for the new age of electricity. Barnard's interest in science, research and theory is obvious in his writing. He was strongly influenced by George Field, whose pigments he praised, as well as the Scottish physicist David Brewster, who had experimented with polarized light and in 1816 invented the kaleidoscope; the mathematician and astronomer John Herschel, who had been researching colourblindness and experimented with early photography; Johann Wolfgang von Goethe and Michel Eugène Chevreul. Goethe's and Chevreul's main works on colour had been published in English translation in the years before Barnard wrote his book. He may also have been one of the few writers who were influenced by Mary Gartside's lesser-known colour blots in her *Essay on Light and Shade* (see pages 50–53), as a plate of 'Contrasts of Colour' (opposite), illustrated with twelve abstract blot-like images, might suggest. Barnard's blots are one of several plates in a chapter 'Contrasts of colour'. They show the effects of colours placed together in a number of combinations, beginning with 'the simplest of contrasts' of black and white in figure 1 and graduating to more complex ones comprising black, white and secondary (figs. 7, 8 and 9) and tertiary colours (figs. 10, 11 and 12). Their main purpose is to encourage students 'to make experiments from which he may draw inferences by himself', meaning to create similar sample colour combinations in the preparation of a painting.

Two plates in the same chapter illustrate simultaneous colour contrasts and here Chevreul's influence is particularly obvious. Each plate depicts a grey ornamental shape against two different coloured backgrounds. The plates are overlaid with a blank page that has been cut horizontally in the middle, so that the reader can look at each colour combination in isolation as they carry out simple experiments that show how the appearance of the grey shape changes in tone when seen against either blue, yellow, orange or green. The neutral grey appears in the complementary colour to the one in the coloured background. In the example shown overleaf, an orange background makes the grey appear blue and a green background results in a reddish grey figure.

108 INDUSTRIALISM TO IMPRESSIONISM – THE LATER NINETEENTH CENTURY

LEIGHTON, BROTHERS.

CONTRASTS OF COLOUR.

PLATE 25.

ORANGE CAUSES THE GRAY TO APPEAR BLUE.

GREEN CAUSES THE GRAY TO APPEAR RED.

LEIGHTON, BROTHERS.

CONTRASTS OF COLOUR.

It would be as well, in experimenting upon these contrasts in large, to place one of the figures cut out of the same gray paper on a ground of white, that it may be used as a reference, and the real colour of the figure may be seen. In the accompanying plates the neutral gray is exactly the same in each diagram, being printed with the same colour. In Plate 29, Fig. the ground colour is yellow; the neutral gray will in this case appear or purple. In Fig. 2, the blue ground will cause the gray on the figure golden orange, although the tone of the gray on the figure deducts from the distinctness of the complementary c Fig. 1, the ground being orange, the figure appears r ground being green, the figure appears red. tried on a large scale, the complement round the edge of the figure; and it colour approaching in some de matic spectrum.

Carrying out t gard to t

and is almost ly painted panorama

THE WONDERFUL RANGE OF COLOURS DERIVED FROM COAL-TAR
Displayed graphically according to groups. [For explanation see DYEING]

Trees and Butterflies Represent Latest Colour Advances

In 1856 the eighteen-year-old aspiring London chemist William Perkin discovered a dye colour that would change the face of fashion and the textile industry. In his quest to derive quinine – a possible medicinal cure for malaria – from coal tar, he stumbled across an aniline substance that turned fabrics a brilliant purple. He called it mauveine, but it was also known as Perkin's Mauve. The inventor had it patented, and the colour quickly became hugely popular and was produced commercially on a large scale in the later nineteenth century. It was effectively the first synthetic, inorganic dye, composed of carbon, hydrogen and nitrogen, and it was an excellent substitute for expensive natural purple dyes, such as Tyrian purple, which was made from sea snails. (Incidentally, Perkins called his new colour Tyrian purple for a while.) Coal tar, a gooey dark substance, was available in great quantities in Victorian London, as it was a waste product from coal gas street lighting. Mauveine became such a popular colour in fashion that a deep shade of it was even used as an alternative to black in mourning dress, after the period of wearing black clothes for the first year after the bereavement (as was proper) had finished.

Mauveine was only the beginning. By the end of the nineteenth century many more dye colours had been created from coal tar, which is one of the reasons why we see so many intensely coloured dresses and other textiles in the later Victorian period. This image (above)

Left: The 'wonderful range of colours derived from coal tar' is depicted on an elaborate family tree.

Above: Not only does this plate show the effects of colour mixing, but the dial-shaped diagram that encompasses it also advises on the appropriate uses of the tints – for 'Backgrounds, Mountains, etc.' (1–4), 'Flowers, Foliage, etc.' (5–12), 'Flesh' and 'Shadows in Flesh, etc' (13 and 18, and 1 and 19), and so on.

from a late-nineteenth-century encyclopaedia shows 'the wonderful range of colours derived from coal-tar' in the shape of a tree. The tree motif may allude to the origin of the raw material coal in fossilised plant matter. Allowing the artist to depict colours in their chemical 'families', the inspiration for this kind of depiction may alternatively have been images of evolutionary trees or diagrams of taxonomical classification that were popular at the time. But either way, it is also simply an image that expresses the excitement of all these brilliant and relatively cheap new colours.

Another coloured plate (above) from the same encyclopaedia revels in recent developments in colour printing. Here the designer, Frederick Oughton, has used the image of a butterfly to graphically illustrate the various stages of three-colour printing. Underneath is a simple but effective semicircular 'colour indicator', which shows the three primaries red, yellow and blue at the base, from which their secondary and tertiary mixtures fan out, followed by 21 further mixed tints on the semicircle's outer perimeters. The indicator is divided into three equally proportioned angles created from each primary colour at the base. The caption advises on which tints to employ for specific uses and areas of an image. As in many eighteenth- and nineteenth-century colour manuals, pigments have been assigned to every tint, in order to make this diagram a practical tool for paint mixing in printing and painting. Beginning with gamboge for yellow, rose madder for red and French blue (an artificial ultramarine) for blue, the outer mixed tints are created, for example, from Prussian blue and brown madder, or terre verte and yellow ochre.

INDUSTRIALISM TO IMPRESSIONISM – THE LATER NINETEENTH CENTURY

Ornamental Colour for Cosmopolitan Tastes

Owen Jones was the designer and architect responsible for the interior polychromatic colour scheme of the Great Exhibition in 1851. In 1856 he further left his mark on contemporary taste with the publication of his *The Grammar of Ornament*. This lavish and expensive volume of design patterns contained 122 chromolithographed plates by royal lithographers Day & Son and reflected the tastes, as well as production methods, of the Victorian era. Many of the largely geometric, flat and brightly coloured designs were inspired by Jones's travels in Greece, Italy, Spain, Turkey and Egypt, giving many of the designs an exotic and oriental feel. Although not strictly a book on colour, it is a masterpiece in colour reproduction and a mirror to the fast-changing tastes and production methods in the age of steam power. In turn, *The Grammar of Ornament* – which has never gone out of print since its first publication – was an inspiration for other writers and designers.

Sir John Gardner Wilkinson's *On Colour and the necessity for a General Diffusion of Taste among all Classes* was published just two years after *The Grammar of Ornament* and its coloured illustrations (see overleaf) bear a striking resemblance to the plates in Owen Jones's design sourcebook. The book's smaller, uncoloured illustrations are woodcuts, while its eight coloured plates are lithographs, executed by West & Co. At least three of the lithographs were carefully hand-coloured. One must assume that author and publisher wanted to achieve the best possible colour representation and ensure that they resembled the high-quality lithographs produced by Jones and Day & Son.

Wilkinson was primarily an Egyptologist who had travelled widely and published many early books on the study of Egyptian culture. He also had a general interest in antiquities and was a collector of Greek vases, which explains his familiarity with aspects of historic design and ornament, including architecture, interiors and garden design.

The subtitle to Wilkinson's book, 'With remarks on laying out dressed or geometrical gardens', explains the stylistic similarities to *Grammar of Ornament*. Formal layouts of ornamental gardens and multicoloured flower beds are depicted in all the coloured plates as abstract shapes and arrangement. At the beginning of the nineteenth century the landscape designer Humphry Repton (see pages 46–47) had discussed the impact of

This page & opposite:
Plates from Jones's influential The *Grammar of Ornament* (first published in 1856), including the luxurious title page (top) and plates depicting Turkish style (bottom) and Medieval motifs (opposite).

INDUSTRIALISM TO IMPRESSIONISM – THE LATER NINETEENTH CENTURY

INDUSTRIALISM TO IMPRESSIONISM – THE LATER NINETEENTH CENTURY 115

Above left: For a gardener, Wilkinson includes surprisingly little green in the design on the frontispiece to his book. The intention is to show 'how green may be used to light up other colours'.

Above right: A geometric pattern showing the layout of seven colours, offered as an example of harmonious colour proportions. Like the frontispiece, this plate demonstrates how little green is needed to make other colours seem more vivid.

colour theory on garden design, but more in respect of light effects, including reflections in water and the use of coloured glass, in garden architecture. Wilkinson, on the other hand, applied geometrical colour designs to equally geometrical flower beds, much like colouring in a flat sheet. Whereas Repton had considered the many subtle varieties of green created by careful planting of shrubs and trees, Wilkinson did not follow in this Picturesque manner, noting that 'artificial grounds can never resemble nature'. He included very little green in his actual garden designs, focussing instead on brightly coloured flowers, stressing the importance of 'proper selection of the colours for harmonious combinations', of which he gave many examples in the last section of his book. Here, green is merely the ground colour to his principal colours blue, red, scarlet, pink, purple, lilac, yellow, orange and white. But this also being a book about taste in general, he explains his dislike of green in other areas: 'I have been particular in censuring the common error of introducing great quantities of green into coloured ornamentation ... It abounds when people become artificial. But in those periods when taste in colour was pure, the primaries were always preferred.' A traditionalist at heart, Wilkinson's comments on green may well have been caused by the numerous green pigments and dyes that had recently been invented, which were used lavishly in wallpaper design and fashion.

The frontispiece of his book (above left) shows a geometric design in red, blue, white, black and green, intended to illustrate how a small amount of one colour can brighten other colours. The design itself was inspired by the border ornaments of Giotto's fourteenth-century frescos in the Scrovegni Chapel in Padua, Italy.

Plates II (above right) and III (opposite), are the most interesting in the book with regard to general colour order, since they show arrangements of

116   INDUSTRIALISM TO IMPRESSIONISM – THE LATER NINETEENTH CENTURY

Above: One of the more theoretical plates in *On Colour*, this plate shows a number of tints (fig. 5) and the effects of certain combinations. Wilkinson is chiefly interested in harmonious/disharmonious arrangements of the colours.

principal colours, referencing a variety of cultures and styles, including Egyptian and Jewish, similar to Owen Jones's approach.

Plate II (opposite, right) is the one where the pattern, in respect of the proportional arrangement of colours, most resembles Jones's ideas of colour in design. Here, and in some of the following diagrams, Wilkinson roughly follows the Newtonian seven-colour spectrum, with black replacing indigo. However, his aim is not to provide one all-encompassing colour diagram that represents his colour theory. The focus is always on the combination of and quantitative relation between colours, whether there are three or seven or more. Again, Wilkinson's notes remark on how a small amount of green brightens the whole design. This is one of the plates coloured by hand in thickly applied watercolour. Plate III (above) shows twelve examples of harmonious or discordant combinations of principal colours, omitting any intricate patterns. What is interesting is that he also includes examples of 'discordant' colour combinations (figs. 6, 7, 8, 9 and 10 on this plate). This 'how not to arrange your design patterns' is conceptually related to Repton's method of showing his client a dull and uninspiring image of their gardens before his proposed improvement.

Wilkinson discusses many other aspects of colour, design and taste, and the book is a curious mixture of philosophical musings, practical advice on colour combinations, colour in classical antiquity and applied to contemporary architecture and design.

INDUSTRIALISM TO IMPRESSIONISM – THE LATER NINETEENTH CENTURY

Immaterial to Material: Bridging the Gap between Science and Art

Right: The purpose of this striking and playful-looking diagram is to allow the reader to discover the 'intermediates' between any two colours, using a piece of glass to reflect one spot on top of another.

Opposite, top: Benson's colour cube is a complex and comprehensive device that visualises his primaries (red, blue and green) at three corners of the cube, with the addition of black, and his secondaries (seagreen, pink and yellow) at the opposite three corners, along with white. On every face, edge and connecting axis are every variation and gradation in between.

Opposite, bottom: Although the cube is intimidating in its complexity, the five plates illustrating the colours found at various sections of it are of an elegant simplicity.

In 1868, the London-based architect William Benson published *Principles of the Science of Colour*. Benson stressed the scientific nature and basis of the book – which was dedicated to the physicist and mathematician George Gabriel Stokes, who had researched fluorescence and ultraviolet light – while aiming to create a colour system that could also be a useful tool in art and design.

Benson's book focuses on material colour – his intention was to help artists to understand 'beautiful' colour arrangements — but he was also concerned with how we translate what we see into physical form; that is, a painting. His colour system was, therefore, based on immaterial colour. In this system, red, green and blue become primaries, yielding the secondaries and complementaries seagreen, pink and yellow. These colours are illustrated (above) as discs on a hexagon against a split black-and-white background.

From these colours Benson developed a complex model to illustrate his system, which was clearly informed by his work as an architect: a tilted 'Cube of Colours' (opposite top). He was the first colour theorist to introduce a cube design to represent a 'natural system of colour', although he does note that it was inspired by a system described in Herschel's *Treatise on Light* from 1830. He also acknowledges Philipp Otto Runge's proposed colour globe from 1810 (see page 144) and Chevreul's efforts. The 'Cube of Colours', depicted early in the book, is uncoloured, but the location of tints and their mixtures are indicated by letters and numbers along the thirteen principal axes. A black-to-white line forms a central axis, with grey at the centre of the cube so that in each cross section of the cube the tints become lighter towards the top and darker towards the bottom. The six colours mentioned above form the corners of the cube, with all other hues located along the axes connecting the main colours. A later edition of the book includes an image of two surface views of the cube with coloured spots indicating the location of 38 hues. Illustrations of the distribution of colours in the sections of the cube are provided in the form of five full-page lithographs (see opposite, bottom) showing groups of coloured spots, all painted by hand, against a heavily inked black printed background except for one of the five plates, which has a background colour of very light brown. There is no lettering on the colour plates themselves,

INDUSTRIALISM TO IMPRESSIONISM – THE LATER NINETEENTH CENTURY

1 Crimson Lake.
2 Vermilion.
3 Chrome yellow.
4. Green.
5. Cobalt Blue.
6. Ultr.ne Blue.
   ARTIFICIAL.

Green.
Blue Green.
Blue.
Ultr. Blue.
Dark Purple.

Purplish Red.
Red.
Orange Red.
Orange Yellow.
Yellow.
Yellowish Green.

Effects produced by mixing pigments.

COMPLEMENTARY COLOURS.

MIXTURE CHART.

Left: Unusual for books of this period, Rood's *Modern Chromatics* included only one coloured plate, and the diagrams on it are simple in their conception.

but the hues are named and identified in tables on their opposite pages. The effort that went into colouring in these spots must have been considerable, as is the case with every hand-coloured colour diagram. The colour spots appear especially intense against the black background and have a timeless abstract appeal.

Just over a decade after Benson published his book, the American physicist Ogden Nicholas Rood published a substantial book on colour science that proved to be tremendously successful in America, Germany, France and English-speaking European regions. *Modern Chromatics, with Applications to Art and Industry* seemed to encapsulate the, by then, very close relationship between art, design, science, commerce and production. Himself a practising painter, mainly in watercolour, Rood was in constant exchange about colour with other artists and his intention was to provide a book of great practical value to artists and designers, as well as those with a general interest in the subject. His interest in optical studies and immaterial colour was perhaps the reason that he was especially well received by Impressionist and Post-Impressionist painters, helped by the almost immediate translations of his work into German and French.

Over 350 densely printed pages, Rood dealt with many aspects of colour and paint, referring to past colour theorists as well as presenting the current state of colour studies. The book's 130 illustrations are small woodcuts, many of them depicting optical experiments, tools or machinery, as well as some simplified diagrams and colour systems. The only coloured plate in the book is the frontispiece (opposite), on which are shown a number of small colour diagrams, including a triangular 'mixture chart', based on the red-green-blue optical system advocated by the scientists Thomas Young and Hermann von Helmholtz. Also included are three colour wheels containing six 'complementary colours' each, and three tables showing the 'Effects produced by mixing pigments', along with a key of numbers assigned to each tint. He also devised a systemic colour wheel, which assigns varying degrees and proportions, or 'angular distances', as he calls them, to the colours, similar to what we saw on Newton's asymmetric wheel from 1704. This was represented as a simple uncoloured line engraving with the names of 22 colours on the unevenly represented radii emanating from a centre. Like Benson before him, Rood derived a material colour system of practical use to artists and designers that was based on spectral colours and optical studies. Although many of his 22 colours bear pigment names, they are also defined by their spectral equivalent, meaning they represent wavelengths. The success of Rood's work lies in his meticulous research and his clear, logical and structured prose style. He was less concerned with complex or aesthetically appealing illustrations of his colour systems.

Vincent van Gogh Immerses Himself in Colour

Above: A surviving palette gives an impression of how Van Gogh painted: the strokes of a broad brush are clearly visible, the arrangement of the paints doesn't seem to follow a particular order and much of the mixing took place on the palette.

Opposite: A self-portrait from 1888 (detail) displays Van Gogh's ideas about colour. The colours are more vivid than life, helped along by a bold interplay of blue and orange complementaries.

Few other artists of the nineteenth century combined such a radical, at times obsessive, approach to the use of colour with an academic interest in colour theory as Vincent van Gogh. Van Gogh was painting in a time when a multitude of new synthetic paints were becoming available, packaged in collapsible metal tubes, ready mixed, some of them cheap, many of them toxic or at least not stable – but always brilliant.

In his colour choices, Van Gogh was not concerned with naturalism but used colour instinctively, as an expression of mood and feeling rather than an accurate depiction of the world around him.

Many of Van Gogh's early paintings (from around 1880–1882) are composed with a predominantly black and brown palette. But in 1882 he announced a change in a letter to his brother Theo: 'As you see, I'm immersing myself in painting with all my strength – I'm immersing myself in colour – I've held back from that until now, and don't regret it.' While we, with good reason, imagine Van Gogh as an impulsive and passionate painter, he was methodical in his approach. He practised the rudimentaries of picturemaking for years, studying artists' manuals and copying the works of the Masters before embarking on his own brief career. Similarly, he was studying colour theory in great depth while painting in those sombre hues, until it was veribly ready to burst out of him. In a letter to Theo from June 1884 he noted that 'The laws of colour are inexpressibly splendid precisely because they are not coincidences.' A few months later he bought himself a copy of Charles Blanc's colour theory *Grammaire des arts du dessin: architecture, sculpture, peinture* (1867) and it is highly likely that he was familiar with other treatises on colour. Blanc's views on colour were critical and thought-provoking. He considered colour an inferior and difficult element of art, something that needed to be either avoided or controlled. Van Gogh was clearly piqued by this and became obsessed not only with colour itself, but also concepts of colour order. He told Theo in November 1885, 'I am utterly preoccupied with the laws of colour. If only we'd been taught them in our youth!'

We see the dramatic shift to the expressive, non-naturalistic use of colour that we associate with Van Gogh's most famous works from around 1886. While this may largely have been triggered by his move to Paris and exchanges with the artistic avant-garde, studying colour literature may also have been a significant factor. He retained his passion for colour throughout the rest of his short life, working feverishly and rapidly on paintings that have now become iconic. Musing on Blanc's writings, he once suggested that 'a painter does well if he starts from the colours on his palette instead of starting from the colours in nature.' In *Self-Portrait as a Painter* (right) from 1888 we can clearly see the pure colour he has squeezed onto the palette, ready to be mixed, wrestled with, enjoyed and transformed into a painting.

Van Gogh often had a very clear idea about the chromatic layout of a painting before applying it to the canvas, and frequently commented on the characteristics of certain pigments. He considered black and white to be colours in their own right, noting that 'their simultaneous contrast is as striking as that of green and red, for instance'. But personal observation, reflection and perception of colour were what informed his paintings more than anything else. Contemplating painting one of his best-known motifs, the starry sky, he said, 'It often seems to me that the night is even more richly coloured than the day, coloured in the most intense violets, blues and greens. If you look carefully you'll see that some stars are lemony, others have a pink, green, forget-me-not blue glow. And without labouring the point, it's clear that to paint a starry sky it's not nearly enough to put white spots on blue-black.'

Palettes as Mirrors: Artists and Their Colours

A palette can be the mirror of an artist's style and personality

As we saw in the example of Vincent van Gogh on the previous page, painters' palettes can tell us much about the materials and pigments available at the time and, perhaps more importantly, about the artist's colour preferences. Sometimes they even give insight into the creation of a specific work of art. Among other things, they reveal how the painter ordered colours for their immediate use in a painting, in a more fluid and organic way than the arrangement of colours and other materials you find in a paint box. In short, a palette can be the mirror of an artist's style and personality, especially when included as an iconographical element in a painter's work. Making visual statements about your choice of materials, studio space and colour preferences in self-portraits is not uncommon and often these painted palettes can provide fascinating information about an artist's painting and colour mixing techniques, as we have seen in the simple but expressive self-portrait of Gabriele Münter on page 6, or William Hogarth's depiction of the palette as the compositional centre of his self-portrait on page 31. As part of the composition of a painting, palettes are frequently attributed a heightened symbolic meaning and can become powerful emblematic tools of self-expression. But palettes are also objects of beauty and design in their own right. There is a solidity and often symmetry to palettes themselves, which is broken up and brought to life by the soft, malleable and constantly changing paints applied to them. Many palettes have acquired an almost fetishist quality, especially when having belonged to a famous and revered artist. They are among the most tactile and intimate of artists' tools. We can gaze at each one and imagine how the artist chose it, prepared it for painting, held it tight during the creative process, then cleaned it and prepared it for its next use.

Opposite: This palette belonging to Eugène Delacroix is conspicuous for its order and restraint, with dabs of subtly varied hues arranged in a precise order.

THE EXEMPLARY PALETTE OF EUGÈNE DELACROIX

On this palette that belonged to the French Romantic painter Eugène Delacroix we find dozens of small patches of pre-mixed paint placed in three orderly rows. The meticulous layout of paint samples gives us an insight in how the artist thought carefully about the colour composition of a painting. Delacroix was known for taking great care and finding joy in mixing new colours and experimenting on palettes to see how they would work when placed next to each other. In his diaries the artist himself confirms what this object reveals. In 1850 he commented on his palette as a source of artistic energy: 'My freshly arranged palette, brilliant with contrasting colours, is enough to fire my enthusiasm.' It is likely that he used this and similarly arranged palettes not for the actual painting process, but instead as a visual template. Delacroix's minutely arranged palettes became objects of desire and admiration in artistic circles. The poet Charles Baudelaire thought they resembled carefully arranged bouquets of flowers, and in 1930 the painter Léon Piot even made them the subject of a 100-page long book, *Les Palettes de Delacroix*.

Above: Less orderly than Delacroix's palette though still beautiful, Edgar Degas' palette is notable for the great quantity of white on its right-hand side.

THE LUMINOUS PALETTE OF EDGAR DEGAS

This palette by the French painter Edgar Degas is of a particularly ergonomic shape that allows the artist to rest it gently in the folds of an arm or on the body. Degas is often described as a typical Impressionist and did indeed form many friendships with Impressionist artists, but he was as much concerned with the careful studying and copying of Old Masters (Dutch and Italian) as he was with painting *en plein air* – in the open, capturing fleeting moments and impressions. He became most famous for painting ballet dancers on stage and behind the scenes, drenching the figures in a luminous light and giving them fuzzy contours to add to the sensation of movement, often depicting them from unusual angles. With regard to composition, he was possibly inspired by early photography; he used colour as a subtle but powerful tool to create a particular sensuousness and brightness. In this he was much influenced by the work of contemporaries he admired, such as Édouard Manet and Eugène Delacroix (see previous page), while developing his own distinctive style. This palette reflects both Degas' spontaneity and discipline: there is a clear order and tidiness to the arrangement of the oils on the board, yet we also see much mixing on the palette and the creation of subtly contrasting tints. The most prominent colour is white, which gives his work its typical luminosity.

CAMILLE PISSARRO'S FIGURATIVE PALETTE

Above: A palette from Camille Pissarro is like a working example of his ideas about colour order. We get the pure pigments arranged around the edge, and a picture demonstrating their use.

Here, we have a quite different palette from the French Impressionist painter Camille Pissarro. It appears to be a playful take on the concept of the painter's palette: the artist's tool has been used as a paint surface carrying a figurative work of art in its own right. Pissarro treats the wooden palette like a canvas, without attempting to incorporate the ergonomic shape of the thumbhole or the curved edges, covering it with a rural scene of peasants with a cart in a field, under an expansive sky. Yet, Pissarro references the intended purpose of the palette by including thick daubs of umixed paint, the colours red, blue and yellow, as well as white, a dark brownish-purple tertiary, and a green that blends into the painted foliage, around the top and side edges of the image. Around the time this palette was created (c. 1878–1880) Pissarro was known to have worked with a reduced range of primary and secondary colours, augmented only by white, so this palette, although an artificial construct, does indeed reflect his personal colour choices and arrangements.

It may look like a whimsical object, but Pissarro was responding to a popular trend among art collectors to buy and commission palettes from established artists, both as an investment and for their decorative value. This particular palette was created for a Monsieur M. Laplace, a restaurateur in Paris. He paid 50 francs for it, which was more than the price of a small canvas by Pissarro, and it is likely that he intended to display it in his brasserie La Grande Pinte. Pissarro excitedly wrote about Laplace's interest in ornamented artists' palettes to Claude Monet, but it is not known whether Monet was ever commissioned to produce a similar object.

ELISABETH LOUISE VIGÉE LE BRUN'S ELEGANT

SELF-PORTRAIT IN A STRAW HAT

Above: Briefly travelling back in time, we can see how in the eighteenth century artists were far more concerned about accurate (albeit emblematic) depictions of life.

In Elisabeth Louise Vigée Le Brun's *Self-Portrait in a Straw Hat*, painted after 1782, we see an artist proudly posing with her palette and brushes. Her pose is idealised and expresses composure, serenity and beauty. There is no attempt to show the messiness of a painter's work or a studio environment; Le Brun depicts herself dressed extremely fashionably. Her costume may appear loose, rustic and slightly casual, but the large earrings and fine fabrics indicate that she is a relatively wealthy, distinguished and successful woman. She is facing the viewer and looking out of the picture, against a backdrop of a landscape with a vague low horizon and a cloudy sky, holding her palette and paint-dipped brushes casually in her left hand while leaning on a column. Everything about this self-portrait is elegant and measured, and the colours on the palette reflect the careful and deliberate composition of the painting, and thus her art in general. Le Brun arranges her colours neatly along the top edge, with white closest to the thumbhole, followed by light shades of yellow, moving to oranges and reds and then darker tints. Two shades of blue, which feature in many of her works, and a pink tint are placed in a second row, close to her thumb. While conveying an image of taste and professionalism, Le Brun also wittily self-references with her palette: the prominent pink shade is very similar to the colour of her dress, and the flowers that are pinned to her straw hat seem to mirror the tints on her palettes almost exactly.

PAUL CÉZANNE'S STRUCTURAL
SELF-PORTRAIT WITH PALETTE

Above: Compared with Le Brun's self-portrait (opposite) Cézanne's painting has a distinctly unpolished feel. But it is vivid and alive, and demonstrates the radical new ideas informing art towards the end of the nineteenth century.

Just over a hundred years later, Paul Cézanne created an almost exact mirror of the colours he favoured, on the palette included in his 1890 *Self-Portrait with Palette*. The sumptuous shades of green that are so prominent in many of his works occupy much of the board, including the top edge, where there is evidence of mixing and creating darker shades of green. It is highly likely the pigments used here were highly toxic emerald green and a chromium-based viridian. Small blots of intense yellow and red paint are placed at either end of the top edge, all against a background of earthy browns and ochres.

Expressive and to a certain extent non-naturalistic in his use of colour, Cézanne was particularly concerned with structure and solidity in his paintings, in stark contrast to many of his Impressionist contemporaries. This self-portrait and the palette within it are perfect examples of achieving a strong visual structure in a painting by combining line and colour masterfully. The solidity of Cezanne's work is represented in his own upright posture and the clear verticals, diagonals and horizontals of his easel and palette, the latter placed at an unnatural but perfect 90-degree angle to the easel and the picture's side edges. The almost geometrically arranged palette is presented full frontal, almost like a painting within a painting, part advertising the painter's art, part forming a defensive shield.

A Rose for Chevreul: Charles Lacouture's *Répertoire chromatique*

Opposite: Lacouture's 'Trilobe synoptique' depicting various mixtures of the primaries red, yellow and blue, including tonal variations.

Overleaf: An elegant colour flower: the twelve petals of the 'Rose synoptique' show different hues and their tonal gradation. The fine protective paper separating it from the title page provides a key to the hues.

At the end of the nineteenth century, the French botanist Charles Lacouture, Professor of Natural History at the University of Metz, published a scientific treatise on colour dedicated to Chevreul's work. Lacouture's *Répertoire chromatique, solution raisonnée et pratique des problèmes les plus usuels dans l'étude et l'emploi des couleurs (Chromatic repertory: logical and practical solution to the most frequent problems in the study and employment of colours)*, published in 1890, is an expensively produced book, comprising 144 pages of text and 29 chromo-lithographic plates, plus additional uncoloured diagrams. Despite his admiration for Chevreul, the author argued that Chevreul's system was not easy to apply by artists, designers, and so on. Lacouture aimed to provide a simplified and extended version of Chevreul's work, in which he would elaborate on factors such as surface finish, materiality of coloured objects and light conditions. We can argue about whether or not Lacouture achieved his aim of making Chevreul's theories easier to understand and apply, but he certainly created an aesthetically impressive new book on colour, with full-page (32.5 x 25 cm) coloured lithographs of the highest quality. Among these are a couple of particularly beautiful and inventive colour diagrams.

The frontispiece is the 'Rose synoptique' (overleaf), a fan-shaped variation on a colour circle, consisting of six principal colours and six mixtures of those. The colours are shaped like flower petals and the saturation increases towards the centre of the diagram, where overlapping triangular shapes are placed. There is no letterpress on the rose, but a key to the diagram, with references to the other colour plates in the book, is printed onto the tissue guard of the frontispiece and can be placed over it.

The second colour plate is Lacouture's 'Trilobe synoptique' (right), which forms a reference diagram visualising the range of mixtures and greyscales of the primaries red, blue and yellow. Unusually, Lacouture did not opt for a conventional representation of overlapping circles. Instead, each primary colour forms a bow or wing shape, with its brightest range along the outer edge of the wing. Interestingly, the darker shades of each tint were not created by changing the colour of the printing ink but the thickness of the fine parallel lines of colour against the white background of the paper.

Despite the ambitious nature of the treatise, it was never translated into other languages and remained influential only in French-speaking circles.

RÉPERTOIRE CHROMATIQUE · Frontispice PLANCHE I^bis

TRILOBE SYNOPTIQUE

N. B. Fermer l'atlas pour soustraire ces planches à la lumière aussitôt qu'on n'a plus besoin d'en faire usage.

Chromolith. C. Severeyns.

RÉPERTOIRE CHROMATIQUE　　　　　　　　　　　　　　Frontispice PLANCHE

ROSE SYNOPTIQUE

N. B. Fermer l'atlas pour soustraire ces planches à la lumière aussitôt qu'on n'a plus besoin d'en faire usage.

Chromolith. G Severeyns.

DIAGRAMME DE LA ROSE SYNOPTIQUE

R	représente	le rouge ;
RO	"	le rouge-orangé ;
O	"	l'orangé ;
JO	"	le jaune-orangé ;
J	"	le jaune ;
JV	"	le jaune-vert ;

V	représente	le vert ;
BV	"	le bleu-vert ;
B	"	le bleu ;
BV	"	le bleu-violet ;
V	"	le violet ;
RV	"	le rouge-violet.

Les chiffres romains désignent les nos des planches qui correspondent aux diverses parties de la rose synoptique.

134 **COLOUR FOR COLOUR'S SAKE** – THE RADICAL EARLY TWENTIETH CENTURY

Colour for Colour's Sake: The Radical Early Twentieth Century

The Impressionist movement of the latter nineteenth century proved a a catalyst for changing not only how we thought about colour, but also how we thought about art in a much wider sense. It was a truly radical movement, upsetting traditional artistic conventions and emboldening artists to push their field's boundaries ever further. The ideas propagated by the French Impressionists spread quickly throughout Europe, and the decades that followed Impression's inception saw a raft of new, related movements, including Post-Impressionism, Expressionism and Fauvism, swiftly follow. Often, these new movements enjoyed only brief lives, but each one left a distinctive mark on the face of the brave new, technicolour world.

Painters not only experimented with pure and intense colours but also wrote about the spiritual and symbolic meaning of colour

Left: A Fauvist colour wheel, of sorts; Henri Matisse created *The Snail* – a huge and joyful example of his cut-out technique – in 1953, only the year before he died.

In the wake of Impressionism, colour became much more than just a necessary aspect of painting (and an inferior one at that, according to classical standards); it developed into a powerful expressive tool. Many early-twentieth-century artists, especially from French and German avant-garde groups, such as Les Fauves and Der Blaue Reiter, freed of the concept that the goal of art was to reproduce reality as beautifully and accurately as possible, made colour a driving force and distinct subject matter of their work.

As with Impressionism, the term 'Fauvism' was coined as a slight by an art critic. Like many of his peers, Louis Vauxcelles objected to the new work shown by Henri Matisse and André Derain at their 1905 salon d'automne exhibition in Paris. Comparing their seemingly incomprehensible modern art to a Renaissance statue that shared the exhibition space, he disparaged Matisse and Derain with the memorable phrase, 'Donatello parmi les fauves,' or 'Donatello among the wild beasts'. The Fauvists were directly inspired by colour theory, particularly the effects of complementary colours. Taking up where Van Gogh and Seurat had left off, they celebrated pure, bright pigments, and, beginning a move towards abstraction, they simplified their subjects, lending the colours themselves even more importance. Fauvism was not a long-lasting movement, as many of the artists involved in its conception soon turned to other things, including the largely monochrome Cubism. Matisse, however, celebrated colour throughout his life.

In Germany, just a few years later, Der Blaue Reiter, a group of painters including Wassily Kandinsky, Franz Marc and Paul Klee not only experimented with pure and intense colours but also wrote about the spiritual and symbolic meaning of colour. The results were important new interpretations of what Goethe and other writers had begun discussing 100 years earlier: the idea that colour signified more than its physical form, and that individual colours might point to distinct meanings.

The aims and innovations of both groups eventually resulted in the creation of the Bauhaus, a group or

school of which both Kandinsky and Klee were members; it embraced new materials and technologies and combined these with a new philosophy of aesthetics, in which colour theory played a big part. Their aim was for minimalism, clarity and functionality.

As the western world continued to become wealthier, and products and paints became increasingly available in wider ranges, the first half of the twentieth century saw an abundance of books published on the use of colour in interior decoration and architecture. It is in this century that we first begin to see books illustrated with coloured photography. The Polish-born British photographer Carl Hentschel had recently invented the new photographic three-colour printing process that would radically change the look, style and quality of illustrated books. Hentschel's method of photographic printing effectively replaced the messy, wasteful and complicated process of woodblock or metal plate printing in colour. While this accurate and exciting new way of copying artists' works led to the rise of the gift book, often in the form of lavishly illustrated travel books and collections of fairy tales and folklore, the new method was at first only cautiously used in books concerned with colour theory. Authors such as the German chemist Wilhelm Ostwald still opted for pasted-in hand-coloured colour chips in his instructive publications in the 1910s and '20s.

In the twentieth century, we still see a number of charts and lists that wouldn't look too out of place in books from centuries past. On the one hand, there were the more experimental schemas, for example Emily Noyes Vanderpoel's beautiful colour analyses. On the other hand, various organisations were attempting to standardise colours for use in manufacturing and industry, and for this purpose a number of expensive colour charts were produced, including one by the newly founded British Colour Council. Smaller and cheaper versions of colour charts were also produced as advertising materials by private companies, in a continuation of the tradition of lists of colours and pigments printed in nineteenth-century books on colour. The paint charts you can pick up today in most shops that sell architectural paint or artists' materials have their origin in the early twentieth century, when advertising became much more aggressive and colour printing became cheaper.

It is interesting that the exponential rise of consumer culture was occurring during a time of intense spirituality, manifesting not only in the intellectual works of Der Blaue Reiter and Bauhaus, but also in

It is in this century that we first begin to see books illustrated with coloured photography

a heightened interest in the paranormal or supernatural, and the popularity of esoteric religious movements such as theosophy. Charles Webster Leadbeater, a key proponent of the latter, made the connection between colour and intangible qualities, which Goethe had been considering in 1799 with his *Temperamenten-Rose* (see page 45), even more literal. Leadbeater's beliefs led him to publish a book that explained the interpretation of auras – colourful emanations of inner qualities – for which purpose he included in his book a table of 25 colours and their specific meanings.

With the outbreak of the Second World War, the western world began to turn away from its fascination with mysticism. Perhaps it seemed more important to focus on practical and material things. But the ideas promoted in the early twentieth century have left a legacy of some of the most fascinating works of art, design and literature the world has ever seen.

Left: Plate XXVI from Charles Webster Leadbeater's *Man Visible and Invisible* (1902) illustrates 'The Causal Body of the Arhat', or the aura of an adept of the Theosophical path. In the text, Leadbeater acknowledges the difficulty in illustrating such an advanced aura, which may be reflected in the larger format of this fold-out plate.

Blots & Grids:
Emily Noyes Vanderpoel

Above: An example of Vanderpoel breaking down a coloured object into its chromatic components: A mummy cloth she has studied comprises 50 parts red, 24 parts green, twenty parts blue and six parts orange.

Opposite: Vanderpoel's plates were printed on high-quality and slightly textured paper, and illustrate a wide range of colour aspects. Here she depicts colour harmonies in a blot-style similar to Mary Gartside and George Barnard in the nineteenth century.

Examples of women publishing on colour in the eighteenth and nineteenth centuries are rare. In the early twentieth century, coinciding with the rise of avant-garde groups, the opening of a number of art colleges for women and the advent of Modernism and Expressionism, women gained a stronger voice, both with their art and in publishing, although men still dramatically outweighed women in public visibility and the intellectual establishment in general. In the very early years of the twentieth century, the New York-born painter Emily Noyes Vanderpoel published an intriguing book on colour: *Color Problems: A Practical Manual for the Lay Student of Color* (1902). Like other women colour writers before her, such as Mary Gartside (see pages 50–53) and Mary Philadelphia Merrifield (see pages 104–105), Vanderpoel was born into privileged circumstances and enjoyed a private education. She was an active member of several societies and organisations that supported women, including the Daughters of the American Revolution and the Litchfield Female Academy, Connecticut, where she lived for most of her life.

Vanderpoel appears to have been widowed young and lost her only son and daughter-in-law around the time of the publication of *Color Problems*, which may explain her sudden and intense publishing output. A chronological list of colour literature at the end shows how widely Vanderpoel had read on the subject: beginning with Leonardo da Vinci, she further lists Goethe, Chevreul, Field, Jones, Rood, Wilkinson and Lacouture, among many others. A number of titles are German and French, and a particular interest in colour vision and colour in other cultures is apparent.

The weighting of text and images in *Color Problems* is almost equal (137 text pages and 117 plates). 'Color cannot be fully appreciated by any written description, the text has been made as brief as possible, the plates full and elaborate,' Vanderpoel explained in her introduction. The plates include some predictable images of the optical range, colour contrast, gradation and tables of complementary colours; others are more experimental. The book even included transparencies, some of them coloured, to be used as overlays. Most plates are highly abstract, such as one illustrating colour harmonies (right) that recalls the colour blots of Gartside and George Barnard (see page 109), while some plates illustrating colour contrasts appear like precursors of Josef Albers's colour squares from *Interaction of Color* (see pages 180–181). A number of freer compositions which she calls 'color notes' resemble Turner's colour notations from his many sketchbooks – simple brushstrokes of no more than a handful of colours, largely based on the observation of nature. For example, 'Color note from a bluebird – A harmony of cobalt and light red', or 'Color note from leaves on a tree – The sun glancing across the smooth leaves makes a cool gray, and shining through them makes a warm green. The shaded leaves are a deep green.'

The most remarkable plates in the book are dozens of 'color analyses', in which Vanderpoel breaks down an image, an object or a design pattern into its chromatic components and presents the resulting colour key on a 10 x 10 square grid, with the proportional distribution of each colour noted below to the total of 100 squares. Vanderpoel's way of visualising colour order and layout was measured, methodical, mathematical and abstract, but also surprisingly simple. It is likely that these images had some influence on the development of abstract art and design in the twentieth century, but as yet the author is under-researched and *Color Problems* is now an extremely rare book.

138 COLOUR FOR COLOUR'S SAKE – THE RADICAL EARLY TWENTIETH CENTURY

PLATE XXXIII

A HARMONY OF ONE COLOR

A HARMONY OF CONTRAST

COMPLEX HARMONY

Albert Henry Munsell's Hue, Value and Chroma

Above & opposite: Three diagrams from Munsell's *Atlas* (1915), detailing a ten-hue system, with notation for chroma and value (Chart H, above); an explanation of 'chroma', or 'the strength of pigment colors' (Chart C, opposite, top) and an explanation of 'value', or 'the amount of light reflected from pigments' (Chart V, opposite, below).

Albert Henry Munsell was an American teacher and artist whose lifetime ambition was to create and perfect a colour system that was easy to understand, accurate, and based on how colour is perceived by humans. He wanted his system to be a useful tool for colour choice, matching and identification, as well as being suitable for teaching at all levels. Although it appears complex, his system was based on the principle that any visualisation of colour order needed to be three-dimensional. Munsell was, of course, not the first to suggest this, but he turned this central idea into a numerical system based on three identifiable and measurable qualities of colour: hue, chroma and value. Hue is the colour or tint itself, to which we could give a name, such as red, yellow blue, and so on. Value refers to the lightness or darkness of a colour. The third attribute, chroma, denotes the saturation or brilliance of a colour. All colours are arranged in relation to a central axis of neutral colours, ranging from white at the top to black at the bottom. The result was a flexible, three-dimensional model in which each colour could be identified by its location on the spatial model, referred to numerically as HVC and known as the 'Munsell color space'.

Munsell introduced his ideas of a colour sphere and colour space in his first publication, *A Color Notation: A Measured Color System, Based on the Three Qualities Hue, Value and Chroma* (1905). This was a short, small format and concise treatise, intended for use in education, and an attempt to standardise colour teaching at school level. Later editions were published with a loosely inserted 'Munsell Student Chart' and a set of 26 coloured 'Munsell chips', for students to arrange on the chart. The early editions of this popular work contained a coloured frontispiece showing a painted colour globe, after a pastel by Munsell, created in 1900 (see page 145). Munsell was also known to have used simple models of colour globes made of tin and wood in teaching, which are the earliest known examples of an actual colour globe. He soon developed his three-dimensional model further, realising that colour space could not be perfectly represented in a spherical form. In all his publications, the symbol of a colour sphere appears as a decorative logo on the covers, but the preferred representation of his colour system is a colour tree, with chromatic branches of different lengths extending from the central neutral trunk (see overleaf).

COLOUR FOR COLOUR'S SAKE – THE RADICAL EARLY TWENTIETH CENTURY

Above & opposite: Although Munsell frequently represented his ideas in the form of a globe (see overleaf), the tree design, represented on these pages as a figurative, traditional-style woodcut (above) and a schematic form (opposite), seems to have been his favoured mode for presenting his ideas about colour.

Munsell's most beautiful and elaborate book, the *Atlas of the Munsell Color System* was published in 1915. Its format was an impressive 29 x 38 cm and it is reminiscent of the ambitious atlas of Chevreul's work published in 1861 (see pages 94–101). Munsell's *Atlas* contains fifteen colour chart plates, some with overlays that can be lifted, for example on Chart V (previous page, bottom), depicting the greyscale 'Axis of the color tree'. The colours are pasted-in squares or spots of coloured paper, similar to the early publications by Munsell's contemporary Wilhelm Ostwald (see pages 166–169). This was certainly an expensively produced book, and the delicacy of the plates is pointed out to the reader. Each one comes with a printed instruction in capital letters at the bottom of the page: 'PROTECT THIS CHART FROM DUST AND HANDLING'.

In 1917 Munsell, whose colour system had quickly been internationally accepted and would become the basis of other colour systems, such as the 1976 CIELAB, founded the Munsell Color Company, but he died just a year later. His son Alexander E. R. Munsell took over the company and continued publishing and promoting his father's work. In 1942, after the sale of the company, the Munsell Color Foundation was established in its place. This was closed in 1983.

A third book authored by Munsell was published posthumously in 1921 by The Strathmore Paper Company. *A Grammar of Color – Arrangements of Strathmore Papers in a Variety of Printed Color Combinations According to the Munsell Color System*, was supposedly prepared by Munsell shortly before his death. It is as much a celebration of his life's work as it is a masterpiece of book design. It looks elegant in its tall oblong format (32 x 22 cm) and is printed on a range of different coloured matt papers produced by the Strathmore Company. It was of course also a great advertising object for the company, who proudly announced that this was 'the first presentation of [Munsell's] system to the Printing, Advertising and Paper Trade'. The decorations and typeface of the introductory text that explains Munsell's colour system and its application to print culture were designed by T. M. Cleland. Cleland was also responsible for the letterpress of the nineteen fold-out colour sheets that follow the text. These tactile sheets were printed with numerous colour combinations, using many of Munsell's by then well-known diagrams.

Copyright 1911 A. H. Munsell

COLOUR INTO THREE DIMENSIONS

From the middle of the eighteenth century, colour theorists began to tackle the problem of how to represent the different dimensions of colour in a colour system. Drawn or painted visualisations of colour systems, such as charts and wheels, struggled for decades to show more than hues and a number of their mixtures. A major problem was how to depict colour saturation, or the amount of black and white in a colour. In his colour wheel from 1704 Isaac Newton intended a third dimension to the diagram by marking a central white point, towards which the spectral colours of his wheel would decrease gradually in intensity of hue (see pages 12–15). In 1810 the German painter Philipp Otto Runge visualised a three-dimensional colour globe with a point of pure black at one pole and pure white at the other, between which all hues developed (right). Other theorists and artists made similar attempts at conveying a three-dimensional system in a two-dimensional medium, with varying degrees of both success and complexity. Mary Gartside, for example, had used the term 'ball' in relation to a colour circle in 1805, suggesting that she wanted the reader to imagine it as a three-dimensional object, while William Benson drew a three-dimensional colour cube in 1868 (see page 119). In the early twentieth century, Munsell used the simplified image of a colour globe as a decorative logo on many of his publications. His fully developed colour system was considerably more complex than this little image, resembling a not perfectly spherical 'colour tree' (see pages 142–145), but the most important aspect was the idea that colour occupied space in several dimensions.

The frontispiece of Munsell's *A Color Notation* (opposite) is an image of a pastel drawing, dated 1900, of an actual colour globe. It looks astonishingly like Runge's etching of a colour ball from 90 years earlier. We know that Munsell used simple models of colour globes, possibly made by himself, in teaching colour theory, and it is highly likely that other three-dimensional models were designed in the eighteenth and nineteenth centuries, but no significant examples survive.

In recent years, a number of creative attempts have been made to produce three-dimensional colour models. Munsell's colour tree, complete with detachable colour chips mounted radially on plastic panes, is available via Pantone®, while in 2011 artists Daniel E. Kelm and Tauba Auerbach created a digitally printed *RGB Colorspace Atlas* in book form. This fascinating object takes the form of a cube (20 x 20 x 20 cm) and presents every variation of the RGB model of colour. The concept of printing RGB is in fact somewhat misleading; reminiscent, in fact of the confusion of material with immaterial colour common to in the eighteenth century. RGB (based on the colours red, green and blue) is an additive model, intended for electronic devices such as computer screens. At some point during the creation of this book, the colours would have been converted to a subtractive model – probably CMYK (based on cyan, magenta, yellow and black) – for printing.

Above: Philipp Otto Runge's theoretical 'Farbenkugel' (colour globe) from 1810, with views of the white and black poles (top, right and left), an 'average through the equator (bottom left) and average between the poles (bottom right).

Right: Munsell's colour globe from 1900, as the frontispiece to *A Color Notation*.

COLOUR FOR COLOUR'S SAKE – THE RADICAL EARLY TWENTIETH CENTURY

PLATE I

A BALANCED COLOR SPHERE
PASTEL SKETCH

Owing to the impossibility of obtaining colours of sufficient depth at the time of printing, the tints marked "Green Blue" and "Ultramarine" are too light for their places in the circle.

Beyond Newton's Disc: New Ideas in Popular Manuals

Apart from theoretical, critical and experimental literature on colour, the turn of the twentieth century saw the publication of a wealth of popular, practical and affordable handbooks on colour in painting. In contrast to manuals on painting from the early nineteenth century, these books were almost exclusively illustrated using lithographic or photographic image reproductions. But while colour printing was now easier and cheaper, some authors bemoaned the limitations and inaccuracy of mechanical colour reproduction. In most of these publications text still greatly outweighed image content, and however simplified the various wheels and diagrams may appear, they often reference complex systems developed in the nineteenth century.

BARRETT CARPENTER'S DISC FOR ARTISTS

One such was the relatively little-known work by Henry Barrett Carpenter, modestly titled *Suggestions for the Study of Colour*, aimed at fine arts students. Barrett Carpenter was the Headmaster of a School of Art in Rochdale in the north of England and he privately published the book in 1915, with a second edition (shown here) appearing in 1923. He gives much practical advice on how to use colour in art but puts even more emphasis on colour theory and systems in general. The majority of the images illustrating concepts of colour contrast, harmony, discord, arrangement and appearance use abstract or semi-abstract shapes, and the first plate – as in so many books on colour – shows a colour wheel.

In his introduction, the author criticises Chevreul and his trichromatic concept of colour (see pages 94–95) and announces that he wrote his book because he felt a need for new and independent studies of colour. While Barrett Carpenter distanced himself from Chevreul's work, he was more complimentary of American physicist Ogden Rood (see pages 120–121) and modelled his own colour system on Rood's 'natural order of colour', where colours scale from light to dark ranging from yellow (nearest to white light) to violet or purple (nearest to black).

Since his chromatic system is based on Rood's table of ten or eleven colours, Barrett Carpenter's colour circle is already more segmented than one based on a pure trichromatic one, and he has added a further four intermediate tints to Rood's ten (orange-yellow, yellow-green, blue-green and cyan-blue), resulting in a fourteen-tint colour circle. Two things are of additional interest in this little guidebook: firstly, the copy pictured here shows telling signs of use by a painter. Smudges of water-based paint and finger marks can be found on many pages but particularly on the colour wheel plate. One can imagine the book placed next to the paint materials of a young art student, the colour circle displayed as a handy reference image. Secondly, the author has acknowledged the limits of colour reproduction in print culture in the early twentieth century. A pasted-in paper strip (similar to an errata slip) under his colour wheel notes: 'Owing to the impossibility of obtaining colours of sufficient depth at the time of printing, the tints marked "Green Blue" and "Ultramarine" are too light for their places in the circle.' Anxious to provide the best possible image of his colour system, Barrett Carpenter was faced with the problem of how to picture colours – some of which he named after pure, deep and brilliant pigments – within the limits of image reproduction of his time.

Left: Barrett Carpenter's colour wheel is based on the colour system of Ogden Rood, albeit with the addition of four extra intermediate tints.

DE LEMOS'S HANDS-ON APPROACH

In 1920 the American artist, designer, lecturer and art teacher Pedro Joseph de Lemos published a substantial and practical self-study course on *Applied Art – Drawing, Painting, Design and Handicraft* (first published in 1920 and reissued in 1933), aimed at a very wide range of readers, ranging from children to teachers. It is not strictly a book about colour, but de Lemos, a dedicated and hands-on educator, decided to place 'Drawing and Coloring' at the very beginning of his book, considering these crucial elements in art and design. He had considerable experience in printing and publishing, having worked for the publisher of his book, the Pacific Press Publishing Association in California, and influenced by Japanese woodblock prints in his own artistic practice. It is no surprise then that the work was richly illustrated in both black and white and colour. The text element is structured as a sequence of very short paragraphs in bullet-point style, punctuated by many illustrations, mostly using lithographic printing methods.

Simplicity and clarity were of utmost importance to de Lemos. On the subject of colour harmony, he proposed a simple system of adjoining or contrasting tints: 'Good Color Harmonies are as follows: yellow and orange, orange and red, red and violet, violet and blue, blue and green, green and yellow; also, red and green, yellow and violet, and blue and orange. If we have a flowerpot in one of the colours, then the flower should be of the other colour.'

Most importantly, he encourages his readers to play with cut-out colour shapes in order to understand how colour works. The first colour plate of the book (right) illustrates this in a simple, playful and accessible way. Instead of a colour wheel he opts for a table of six colours (red, orange, yellow, green, blue and violet), typical of a trichromatic system, and adds examples of so-called 'harmony birds' sitting on a branch. These are cut-out shapes of coloured paper, which the reader should use to experiment with colour combinations. Underneath the birds are shown cut-out pieces of transparent coloured paper in the shape of lanterns, which illustrate colour mixtures. This, along with many other plates in the book, is an inventive way of applying colour theory that makes it easy to understand for children, amateur artists and teachers alike.

Above & opposite: Later in his book, at the 'Academic Grades' stage of the course, de Lemos introduces a number of colour wheels and diagrams, some designed to instruct his students on colour harmony, others on colour mixing, matching and symbolism.

1	Red
2	Orange
3	Yellow
4	Green
5	Blue
6	Violet

HARMONY BIRDS

Yellow, Red, and Blue Tissue-paper Lanterns placed over each other on the window will show other colors..

A RAINBOW HARMONY

THE PERSPECTIVE OF COLOUR

Red

Foreground   Middle distance   Distance   Far distance

Purple

Foreground   Middle distance   Distance   Far distance

Violet

Foreground   Middle distance   Distance   Far distance

Yellow-green

Foreground   Middle distance   Distance   Far distance

PLATE IV

Left: Plate IV: 'The Perspective of Colour', showing how the intensity of a hue diminishes as the object recedes into the distance.

Above: On the left, Plate XXX: Jacobs's 24-colour spectrum and, on the facing page, Plate XXXI: 'Colour Types', which shows combinations of different inks.

MICHEL JACOBS'S PLANETS IN SPACE

Michel Jacobs's manual *The Art of Colour* from 1923 is similar in approach to de Lemos's instructive guidebook and aimed at a wide and general readership of amateurs and students of art. Colour knowledge is here applied to many disciplines, including weaving and textile design, fashion, landscape painting and even gardening. In the foreword Jacobs notes that this 'is not a scientific book but is based on scientific knowledge', which explains the short but informed introduction to colour theory in the first chapter. He uses a simple colour wheel as a guideline, based on the spectrum primaries red, green and violet (following Thomas Young's and Hermann von Helmholtz's theory, based on their discovery of optical receptors) but explains that the 'painter's palette need only consist of three colours and white, namely crimson, lemon yellow and blue', from which all other colours can be mixed.

Jacobs was born in Canada but relocated to the United States in 1914, where he worked as an art teacher. An artist and printer himself, he illustrated his book with many of his own works and put particular emphasis on the possibilities of printing in colour in the early twentieth century. Surprisingly though, he criticises the often obvious 'lack of coordination between the colour-printer, the plate-maker and the photographic material concerns', especially in America (where the book was first printed). It is clear that Jacobs put a lot of effort into the 43 illustrations of his book, and while they are not of the greatest technical quality by today's standards, they are a valiant attempt at highlighting the importance of accurate colour reproduction in print culture.

Many of the plates also show considerable creative thinking where colour systems are concerned. Plate IV (opposite), for example, illustrates 'The Perspective of Colour', or how colours change their appearance depending on their distance from the viewer, which suggests how a painter should depict coloured objects in the foreground, middle distance or far distance of a composition. Jacobs provides examples of colour balls like planet formations in red, purple, violet and yellow-green, diminishing in saturation and size with increasing distance.

COLOUR FOR COLOUR'S SAKE – THE RADICAL EARLY TWENTIETH CENTURY

In several other abstract plates Jacobs provides a breakdown of how different inks can be combined in two-, three- and four-colour printing (previous page, top), followed by a pictorial example of progressive proofs of four-colour printing, depicting Adam and Eve in the garden of Eden (above and opposite, top).

Jacobs uses mostly his own paintings to illustrate aspects of colour in art, for example in 'The Violet Veil' (Plate XIX, opposite, bottom left), which is composed of 'split complementaries of five colours and one mutual complementary: blue-green, blue, blue-violet, violet-purple and orange'. However, in his chapters on applied arts, such as costume design and interior decoration, he also borrows from other sources to highlight the adaptability of his colour system. 'Colour in clothes also affects our character,' he states in Chapter 14; and while he recommends a predominantly monochrome palette for men's clothing, he suggests a long and detailed list of different styles and colour combinations for women, according to the time of day, season and social circumstances. He adds an intensely bright picture lifted from a fashion catalogue, showing three young women, one dressed in red, one in orange with a green sash and collar, and one in a deep blue, with 'shadows going toward their complementary' (opposite, bottom right).

The book finishes with an extensive 'Dictionary of Colours', possibly of US-American origin, which lists pigments and describes their places in the spectrum, their complementaries, history, chemical properties and psychological or symbolic meaning.

152   COLOUR FOR COLOUR'S SAKE – THE RADICAL EARLY TWENTIETH CENTURY

Left & above: Here, Jacobs illustrates the advantages of dividing the spectrum into four colours instead of three, for the purpose of lithographic printing. He traces the creation of the image of Adam and Eve backwards through the print process.

Right: Two plates from a section of *The Art of Colour* applying Jacobs's theory to art (left) and fashion (right).

COLOUR FOR COLOUR'S SAKE – THE RADICAL EARLY TWENTIETH CENTURY   153

Plate 1

The effects of light upon a series of commonly used water colors. The left half was kept in the dark, the right half was exposed for two years to studio illumination.

Plate 11

The effect of a polluted atmosphere (essentially the effect of hydrogen sulphide) upon a series of oil pigments. The left hand portions of the painted boards were sealed under glass; the right hand portions, exposed. The pigments from top to bottom of the plate are:

1—Zinc white
2—Flake white
3—Cadmium yellow
4—King's yellow
5—Harrison red
6—American vermilion
7—Chinese vermilion
8—Scarlet vermilion
9—Chrome orange
10—Emerald green
11—Vert emeraude
12—Terra verde
13—Cobalt blue
14—Ultramarine
15—Chrome green (*a mixture of chrome yellow with Berlin blue*)
16—Permanent green (*a mixture of zinc yellow with vert emeraude*)
17—Mars yellow
18—Mars red
19—Mars violet

Martin Fischer's Decaying Palette

Left, top: One of four coloured plates, this shows the fading effect of light on watercolour.

Left, bottom: Another plate shows the effect of 'a polluted atmosphere (especially the effect of hydrogen sulphide) on a range of pigments.

In 1930 the American scientist Martin Fischer wrote a handbook and reference work that dealt almost exclusively with painting tools, techniques and the permanence of pigments, *The Permanent Palette*. In his book Fischer identifies several external causes for pigment change: exposure to light and to air, mixing colours (that is, chemical reactions between pigments and binders), reaction to the paint medium and painting ground, reactions to extreme temperatures, as well as atmospheric pollution. While most of these factors were already known to researchers, there had never before been a publication that dealt exclusively with the permanence of colour.

Fischer saw the need to publish on the instability of artists' materials because he had noted a significant decline in the colour quality of paintings in the nineteenth and twentieth centuries. His book begins with a quote by the Swiss painter Arnold Böcklin, who laments that 'modern pictures have not lasted as those of the old masters have lasted centuries'. It is a modern malaise, so Fischer argues himself, and with an overtly conservative tone he accuses contemporary and recent artists of putting too much emphasis on the 'expression of his emotion in painting', resulting in an impatience concerning the careful choosing and preparation of materials. Sellers of artists' materials and teachers, too, are criticised by Fischer, as being interested only in results, not in good methods. Ready-made materials and lack of knowledge of how grounds are prepared and pigments bound and mixed led to many paintings after 1800 having decayed within a very short span of time, he claimed, citing the dullness of works by James Abbott McNeill Whistler and Frank Duveneck as examples. Given its scientific content and Fischer urging potential readers to engage more with raw artists' materials, it proved hard to find a publisher for *The Permanent Palette*. One rejection letter from 1929 points out that it is 'too scientific in character to hold painters' and that 'it is almost impossible to get artists to take time or make the effort to undertake serious study of colour'.

Two of the four colour plates in the book illustrate pigment use in works of art. The other two are lithographic reproductions of photographic images that make a valiant attempt at showing the effect of light exposure on strips of watercolour (Plate I, opposite, top) and of atmospheric pollution on nineteen oil pigments (Plate II, opposite, bottom). While the lithographs are not entirely successful in showing discolouration, they display an unintended abstract beauty and are good examples of experiments carried out by Fischer in his studio.

Fischer owned a meticulously classified and labelled collection of nearly 300 pigments, dye and binder samples and kept notes and lecture transcripts, all of which were donated to the geological collection at Milwaukee Public Museum after his death. The collection includes the panels of oil paints he tested for fading that are reproduced in *The Permanent Palette*, a postcard from German fellow-scientist Wilhelm Ostwald (see pages 166–169) to Fischer and a complete Ostwald colour wheel, recreated in powdered pigments. It is tempting to think of Fischer as a twentieth-century American version of nineteenth-century British colourman George Field (see pages 60–67), who was equally concerned with the quality of pigments. Like Field, Fischer made an unprecedented impact on the pigment industry of his country. In contrast to Field, though, he made it clear that he was working strictly within the context of fine art and artists' tools only, without developing or promoting any particular colour theory or system.

Orphism: Colourful Music and Musical Colour

The Bohemian-born painter and illustrator František Kupka studied and worked in Paris from 1896. He had a great interest in theosophy, mysticism and colour theory and began making colour the subject of many of his works in the early years of the twentieth century. In his self-portrait from 1907, *The Yellow Scale*, the artist is immersed in the titular colour, visually and symbolically, while the title of a semi-abstract female nude from 1909, *Planes by Colors, Large Nude*, reveals his focus on colour as the dominant compositional tool. In 1909, Kupka read the newly published *Manifesto of Futurism* and was influenced by the ideas coming out of the Futurist movement as well by Cubism, which he encountered at almost the same time. From this point Kupka embraced abstraction and began to produce paintings that referenced colour theory and its relationship with music and movement.

In 1912 he painted *Disks of Newton (Study for a Fugue in Two Colours)*, in direct reference to Isaac Newton's experiments in splitting white light (see pages 12–17). *Disks of Newton* features the seven prismatic colours identified by Newton as well as white, and there is a complete absence of black. The result is a canvas of vivid colours that look utterly infused with light. In the circular arrangement of these pure hues, Kupka plays on the format of Newton's diagram, adding a powerful sense of rhythm and movement, and creating a convincing impression of wheels spinning in bright white light.

Kupka's work almost certainly influenced the much wider known Ukrainian-French artist couple Robert Delaunay and Sonia Delaunay, who joined Kupka in reintroducing pure, spectral colour to the muted and monochromatic palettes favoured by the cubists, as well as pushing cubism towards greater abstraction. Like Kupka, the Delaunays were deeply interested in colour theory, particularly the work of Michel-Eugène Chevreul, as well as spiritual and musical aspects of colour. Robert Delaunay's *Simultaneous Contrasts: Sun and Moon* (1912–1913), for example, is a response to Michel-Eugène Chevreul's *On the Law of the Simultaneous Contrast of Colors* from 1839 (see page 90–91). The Delaunays became the champions of the Orphism, the name for the movement as coined by the French poet Guillame Apollinaire in reference to Orpheus, the musical artist-poet of Greek myth.

Orphism drew a connection between the unrelatedness of music to anything but itself, and the intangible, optical quality of colour as a quality or property. The Delaunays' compositions, like Kupka's, are full of discs, curving lines and colour combinations that give each canvas a distinct rhythm, totally abstracted from reality. Yet though the connection between colour and music was a driving force in Orphist work, it was not as literal as the one Newton drew: 'the chromatism of music and the musicality of colours have only metaphorical validity,' Kupka admitted.

Right: Robert Delaunay's *Rythme n°1* from 1938 has a greater sharpness and clarity than his works from the 1910s but is still occupied with the same themes, with colour, music and movement as the interrelated subjects. Several prismatic colour ranges, along with achromatic tonal ranges, are incorporated in the square composition.

Opposite: Kupka's *Disks of Newton (Study for 'Fugue in Two Colors')* from 1912.

COLOUR FOR COLOUR'S SAKE – THE RADICAL EARLY TWENTIETH CENTURY

COLOUR FOR COLOUR'S SAKE – THE RADICAL EARLY TWENTIETH CENTURY

Mystical Colours: Hilma af Klint and Charles Leadbeater

Left: The pure colours and distinct forms are among the most striking aspects of Hilma af Klint's *Altarpiece No.1* (1915). The sun shape atop a prismatic pyramid suggests both spirituality and Newton's optical experiment.

The Swedish artist Hilma af Klint is often described as a pioneer of abstract painting but her work has, until recently, not been well known or researched. This is partly due to the artist deciding not to show any of her abstract works during her lifetime. She even requested for these not to be displayed until twenty years after her death, which explains why her work is not mentioned in many accounts of Modernism, abstraction and women's art. Born into an educated, bourgeois and Protestant family, she studied art at the Royal Academy of Fine Arts in Stockholm. Her early work was strictly representational and included landscapes, flower studies and portraits.

From a young age she developed an interest in esoteric literature, occultism and spiritualism and in 1880 joined the Theosophical Society. She was at some point mentored by the head of the German branch of the Theosophical Society, Rudolf Steiner, who had worked as the editor of a major scholarly edition of Goethe's works (the 'Kürschner' edition) at the Goethe Archives in Weimar. In 1896 she formed the group De Fem (The Five) with four other female artists interested in experiencing and expressing the mystical and spiritual in their meetings and their art. A séance attended by the group in 1904 was of particular significance for af Klint, as a spirit supposedly instructed her to paint 'the immortal aspects of man'. She began painting canvases on a monumental scale – some of them taller than six metres. Her abstract compositions combine sharp geometric shapes with spirals and intertwined lines that bear some resemblance to climbing flowers. Sometimes recognisable symbolic objects or creatures, for example a shell, a dove or a swan, are incorporated. In one of her series, *Evolution*, naked human figures fill the geometric shapes, reminiscent of Leonardo da Vinci's *Vitruvian Man*. Af Klint's colours are bright, comprising mostly primaries and secondaries. They are often complementary, but sometimes deliberately jarring; for example, combining deep blacks and highly saturated reds, yellows and oranges with dusty pinks, pale blues and muddy browns.

For af Klint, colour became a main means of both creating visible brightness and expressing the invisible and the spiritual. In many of her large abstract works she depicts a full spectrum in shapes and forms that bear a strong resemblance to colour diagrams of the eighteenth and nineteenth centuries. Colour wheels appear in several variations in her art, as do rhombic and triangular shapes. A canvas from *The Dove* series (*No. 14, Group IX/UW*, 1915) shows a large circle of the seven rainbow colours against a black background, while the inside of the circle is white, with a miniature colour wheel in the centre. It is clear that she had considerable knowledge of optical studies and was possibly referring to Newton, Goethe and other colour theorists in her work.

The depiction of the Newtonian colour range is particularly obvious in her series *Altarpieces* (1915). In *Altarpiece No.1* (opposite) Newton's seven colours form a pyramidal shape whose base commands the width of the canvas. All the colours pale towards white as they reach the black, triangular tip of the triangle, which intersects a circlular formation. The innermost circle is coloured gold, and rayed with yellow and violet/pink, in a form suggestive of the sun. The composition is, of course, immediately suggestive of Newton's prism experiment, but it also calls to mind the loaded polarity of Goethe. A deep and even black forms the background: the themes of colour, light and darkness are placed here in a strongly mystical and religious context. Af Klint rightly deserves her reputation as a pioneering abstract artist using colour as a powerful symbolic tool.

THE COLOURS OF MAN

While we don't know which historical colour theories af Klint may have consulted, we do know that she was familiar with the work of two leading British theosophists: Charles Webster Leadbeater and Annie Besant. In 1901 Besant and Leadbeater jointly wrote the book *Thought-Forms: How Ideas, Emotions and Events Manifest as Visible Auras*, which discusses the colour of auras. They proposed that 'emotional changes show their nature by changes of colour in the cloud-like ovoid, or aura, that encompasses all living beings'.

The following year, Leadbeater published his own work on the subject: *Man Visible and Invisible: Examples of Different Types of Men as Seen by Means of Trained Clairvoyance*. The book's frontispiece (left) is a table of 25 colours, each assigned a character trait, or disposition, such as high spirituality, fear, jealously or sensuality.

Leadbeater devoted a chapter to the meaning of colours surrounding astral bodies, and explained the complexity of representing and translating these auras: 'Before we can intelligently study the detail of these various bodies, we must familiarize ourselves with the general meaning of the various shades of colour in them, as indicated in our frontispiece. It will be realised that almost infinite variety is possible in their combination . . . [h]uman emotions are hardly ever unmixed, and so we have constantly to classify or to analyse indeterminate hues in the formation of which many factors have played their part. Anger, for example, is represented by scarlet, and love by crimson and rose; but both anger and love are often deeply tinged with selfishness, and just sofar as that is the case will the purity of their respective colours be dimmed by the hard brown-grey which is so characteristic of this vice.' He discusses black, red, brown, greenish-brown, grey, crimson, orange, yellow, green, grey-green and blue in some detail, but assigns to green the widest range of manifestations.

Twenty-three further colour plates and three diagrams illustrate the appearance of the aura and astral bodies, depicted as ovoid shapes with fluid masses, swirls and blots of colours, with the outline of a male human figure at the centre. The mostly abstract compositions, in which colour and form carry heavy symbolic meaning, bear a resemblance to af Klint's work, and it is likely that Leadbeater's publications influenced her art. The illustrations were created by Count Maurice Prozor, whom Leadbeater thanks at the beginning of the book, while he also expresses gratitude to 'Miss Gertrude Spink, who spent many days in patiently copying them with the air-brush, in order that they might be more successfully reproduced by the photographic process.'

With their focus on spirituality, mysticism and the symbolic meaning of colour Leadbeater's and Hilma af Klint's work predates Wassily Kandinsky's hugely influential 1911 publication *On the Spiritual in Art* (see overleaf). Theosophy as a philosophy had (and still has) a considerable following, and with its focus on spiritual and abstract concepts it was particularly applicable to the arts. It can be argued that the functional abstraction employed in the illustrations of Besant's and Leadbeater's publications appealed to early twentieth-century abstract and expressionist artists and bear a remarkable resemblance to compositions by the Russian Constructivists and the formal geometry of many designs by artists of the greater Bauhaus circle. In fact, Kandinsky, who had a great interest in theosophy without ever becoming actively involved with the Theosophical Society, owned a German edition of *Thought Forms*. Like af Klint, he also met with and studied the writings of Rudolf Steiner, who lectured extensively on spiritual and moral concepts of colour between 1914 and 1924. Steiner's edition of Goethe's *Farbenlehre* is still in print, which suggests that the connections between art, colour literature and theosophical philosophy remain strong.

COLOUR FOR COLOUR'S SAKE – THE RADICAL EARLY TWENTIETH CENTURY

Opposite: The frontispiece to *Man Visible and Invisible*, featuring 25 colours that can be perceived in auras. Each colour is assigned a character trait or emotion.

Above: A figure described as 'The Devotional Type' with a 'most prominent feature' of 'unusual development of the blue, showing strong religious feeling'.

Right: Later in the book, Leadbeater illustrates the aura of 'The Developed Man', a person who has made spiritual progress and has achieved an evenly balanced state of mind. The figure's 'glorious iridescent film is now filled with the most lovely colours, typifying for us the higher forms of love, devotion and sympathy, aided by an intellect refined and spiritualised, and by aspirations reaching ever towards the divine.'

COLOUR FOR COLOUR'S SAKE – THE RADICAL EARLY TWENTIETH CENTURY

From Blue to Infinity: Wassily Kandinsky and the Forms of Colours

The Russian artist Wassily Kandinsky published his treatise *Über das Geistige in der Kunst (Concerning the Spiritual in Art)* in 1911. It became one of the most influential commentaries on abstraction and colour symbolism in European avant-garde art, written by one of its key figures. As colourful and large-scale as Kandinsky's art was, this publication was modest in design and scope. It was of small format (22 x 18.5 cm), bound in plain wrappers, and its 125 pages of text were illustrated with only eleven uncoloured woodcuts made by Kandinsky himself, including the cover image (opposite). The simplicity was deliberate and underlined one of Kandinsky's key ideas: that complex themes in art could be reduced to simple compositions comprising just a few lines, geometric shapes and pure colours. The treatise was surprisingly popular. Further editions were printed within weeks (the 1912 second edition is shown here) and a first English translation by Michael T. H. Sadler was published in 1914.

Kandinsky's system of colour order bears similarities to Goethe's notion of a polarity of blue and yellow, representing darkness and light and cold and warmth. He was also influenced by the German scientist Karl Ewald Konstantin Hering, who had rejected trichromatic colour systems by theorists such as Thomas Young, James Maxwell and Hermann von Helmholtz, and from 1878 proposed his theory of colour vision based on dualistic oppositions (Hering's pairs were red and green, blue and yellow, and black and white).

A recurring theme among artists and writers in the early twentieth century, and especially those experimenting with abstraction, was the correlation between shape and colour. Kandinsky expressed this idea in his publications and later in his teaching, devoting an entire chapter in *Concerning the Spiritual in Art* to 'The Language of Form and Colour'. He probably first encountered the concept through the early abstract painter and teacher Adolf Hölzel in Munich. Kandinsky himself formulated different associations to Hölzel between specific colours and shapes, and later developed this part of his colour theory in surveys he conducted at the Bauhaus art school where he taught between 1922–1933: 'A triangle filled in with yellow, a circle painted blue, a green square, another triangle in green, a yellow circle, a square in blue, these are different forms that have separate distinctive effects,' he wrote.

Right: A woodcut illustration depicting Kandinsky's dualistic colour system that pairs yellow with blue, red with green and purple with orange. The caption beneath it reads: 'The opposites as a ring between two poles = the life of the simple colours between birth and death. (The Roman numerals represent the pairs of opposites.)'

Opposite: The simple cover of Kandinsky's treatise, *On the Spiritual in Art*.

KANDINSKY

ÜBER DAS GEISTIGE IN DER KUNST

ZWEITE AUFLAGE

Right: Kandinsky's design for the cover of *The Blue Rider* almanac from 1912.

Opposite: Kandinsky's *Einige Kreise* (*Several Circles*, 1926), which places overlapping circular shapes against a black background, allude to the relationship between light, darkness and colour. The effect is that of pulsating colour forms interacting. Here, Kandinsky is clearly playing with ideas of the multidimensionality of colour.

Kandinsky had allegedly worked on the book for roughly a decade, which ties in with the course of his path from representational art to near complete abstraction. The year it was finally published was also the year he co-founded the artists' group Der Blaue Reiter (the Blue Rider) in Munich, together with Franz Marc, Gabriele Münter, Alexej von Jawlensky, Marianne von Werefkin, August Macke and other associated artists, such as Lyonel Feininger and Albert Bloch. Inspired by Post-Impressionists, Vincent van Gogh in particular, medieval as well as folk art, and primitivism, they shared an interest in abstraction, new forms of expression and unconventional ways of using colour.

The name chosen for the group, the title of a painting by Kandinsky from 1903 showing a horseman in a blue coat on a white horse in a landscape, reflects the significant role that colour played in their art and philosophy. Blue was both Kandinsky's and Marc's favourite colour and became a key motif in their work. Kandinsky especially considered blue to be the colour of spirituality, masculinity, purity and infinity: 'The deeper the blue the more it beckons man into the infinite, arousing a longing for purity and the supersensuous. It is the colour of the heavens just as we imagine it, when we hear the word heaven.' Yellows, by comparison, were considered feminine, while reds and blacks were used to depict passion, violence and conflict. More radically than anyone before them, Blue Rider artists used colour as an expressive tool and a compositional element in both representational and abstract pictures.

COLOUR FOR COLOUR'S SAKE – THE RADICAL EARLY TWENTIETH CENTURY 165

Science and Maths in a Complex Colour System

Friedrich Wilhelm Ostwald was a Baltic-German scientist who turned his interest to the fine arts, and in particular to colour theory, after receiving the Nobel Prize for Chemistry in 1909. As an amateur painter he made his own pigments and paints, and he published a small practical guidebook entitled *Malerbriefe* in 1904. An English translation, *Letters to a Painter*, appeared in 1907. The *Letters* combined his artistic aspirations with his interest as a chemist in pigment quality and stability. While lecturing chemistry at Harvard University in the United States in 1905/6, he met and was greatly inspired by Albert Henry Munsell (see pages 140–145), whom he followed in his systematic approach.

Ostwald published his first book on colour theory, *Die Farbenfibel* (*The Colour-Primer*) in 1916, followed in 1918 by an extended treatise on the same subject *Die Harmonie der Farben* (*The Harmony of Colours*). Both were small-format and slim volumes that appear simple in design, deceptively like school exercise books, but Ostwald's system is complex, combining geometry and maths, and has been known to baffle even experts in the field. Although manufacturing industries were keen on a standardised colour system, there was some resistance to the idea from traditionalist and craft circles. At one point Ostwald's system was even banned in Prussia.

Nevertheless, the *Farbenfibel*, was a successful publication and went into sixteen editions until 1944, found a readership outside the German speaking world, and was mentioned in *Wilson's Colour Chart* from 1938, despite having by then been superseded by other systems, including Munsell's. Among artists it was particularly popular with the Dutch De Stijl movement, who saw the aesthetic appeal of the strict geometry of the illustrations and the idea of black and white as distinct elements of colour harmony.

Ostwald argued for dividing colours into three basic groups, a concept similar to Munsell's hue, value and chroma. He noted neutral colours, which denote the greyscale between black and white; full colours (or hues), without any black or white; and mixed colours of hues with grey or black content. Informed by Leonardo da Vinci and Karl Ewald Konstantin Hering, Ostwald proposed not three but four 'basic colours': yellow, red, ultramarine and sea green. From these four colours he developed a 24-grade circle of 'standard of hues' (right). He determined a total number of 100 hues on his colour wheel, as indicated by numbers on the inside of the ring, but only the 24 'standard' ones are shown, in the form of pasted-in colour chips.

His system orders colour by the amount of white or black added to the pure colours represented on the wheel, allowing precise mixtures to be recorded in a numeric formula recording colour content, whiteness and blackness. Ostwald represented this in a triangular shape (see overleaf), while a rhomboid device allowed him to depict complementary colours; that is, those appearing opposite on the wheel.

Colour harmony and contrast are other main themes of the book. Ostwald included several pages of examples of colour pairs and trios, represented (respectively) as square or cubic diagrams, the latter used to illustrate the cover of *Farbenfibel*. The illustrations are consistently simple in design but

Opposite: Ostwald's colour wheel demonstrates his tetrachromatic colour order, based around the hues yellow, red, ultramarine and sea green.

— 19 —

ganze Zahl abzurunden. Für 31¼ schreiben wir also 31 und 63 für 62½. Die Farben des achtteiligen Kreises von S. 14 erhalten

77 bis 100. (Die Zählung beginnt bei dem Farbton 00 und läuft im Sinne des Uhrzeigers.)

derart statt der Zahlen 00, 12½, 25, 37½, 50, 62½, 75, 87½ die Zahlen 00, 13, 25, 38, 50, 63, 75, 88 zugeordnet.

2*

Above: One of Ostwald's hues, broken down on a pyramid structure, into intermediates based around a tonal scale.

high in quality: each hue is represented as a small square and either set in a black outline or against a completely black square. The colour squares are not painted or printed but cut out from coloured paper or card produced by Ostwald himself (as he proudly notes in the foreword) or under his supervision, ensuring the most accurate colour depiction. To allow his readers to isolate certain colour squares or to see them against a different coloured background, the book has a small square template cut out of green cardboard, attached to a silk string and incorporated into the binding. It is not known why Ostwald chose this particular colour for the template, but we might assume it was because he considered it neutral, or sufficiently different to black or white.

Although criticised for his complex system, Ostwald proved hugely influential in colour education and spent the rest of his life developing his theories. He continued to publish illustrated books on colour, including several colour atlases. In the 1930s Winsor & Newton published a simplified version of Ostwald's system in English, written by J. Scott Taylor – *The Simple Explanation of the Ostwald Colour System*. This short treatise (51 pages) is described as a handbook that 'has been written to supply the demand which has arisen, both in Great Britain and America, for a small explanatory work on the Ostwald Colour System'. It contains six lithographed illustrations. Ostwald's 24-hue colour wheel and his bar of eight shades of 'achromatic' greys form the frontispiece and are the only coloured plates. As in the original work, the hues are pasted-in squares of coloured card, here 'executed with Winsor & Newton's Ostwald's Standard Showcard Colours'.

In 1969 Faber Birren rekindled an interest in Ostwald when he republished an edited English-language version of the *Farbenfibel* in America as *The Color Primer: A Basic Treatise on the Color System of Wilhelm Ostwald*, along with *A Grammar of Color: A Basic Treatise on the Color System of Albert H. Munsell* and a treatise written by Birren himself, *Principles of Color: A Review of Past Traditions and Modern Theories of Color Harmony*.

168 COLOUR FOR COLOUR'S SAKE – THE RADICAL EARLY TWENTIETH CENTURY

Above: On the left, Ostwald's 'achromatic scale' (unbunt) of eight shades from white to black, and on the right a range of his 'chromatic' (bunt) colours, with the square template on a silk string.

Right: On the left, simple examples of colour contrast and interaction, and on the right Ostwald gives examples of 'three-tone' (Dreiklang) colour combinations, where each hue is at a 33.3-degree distance to the others on the colour wheel.

COLOUR FOR COLOUR'S SAKE – THE RADICAL EARLY TWENTIETH CENTURY

Paul Klee and the 'Chromatic Keyboard'

'Colour and I are one. I am a painter.'

Opposite: Paul Klee's painting *Alter Klang* (*Ancient Harmony*, 1926) is an example of Klee associating colour arrangements with musical arrangements, and of his preferred visual composition of colours like geometric building blocks.

The Swiss-German painter Paul Klee was born into a musical family and was an accomplished violinist even as a young boy, but despite his musical leanings he chose to study art. In 1898 he travelled to Germany to study at the Academy of Fine Arts in Munich. Munich was then an important centre of the arts, rivalling Paris as a place where avant-garde groups congregated and exhibited. Impressionism, Symbolism and Art Nouveau/Jugendstil were the prominent styles and movements of the period, but by 1911 other styles such as Post-Impressionism and Expressionism had developed from these, moving towards abstraction and using colour as an expressive tool and for its own sake.

In Munich, Klee saw exhibitions showing work by Paul Cézanne and Vincent van Gogh and was greatly impressed. There was also the powerful presence of Wassily Kandinsky, who founded Der Blaue Reiter group in Munich in 1911 (see pages 162–165), with which Klee was loosely associated. On visits to Paris around the same time he met Robert Delaunay (see page 156), whose compositions of abstract geometric colour forms had the most direct influence on him. Klee's early work was representational, though with strong abstract tendencies, but after these encounters he began thinking and painting in concepts of colour order and harmony and composed pictures of completely abstract colour planes and shapes. In 1910 he remarked that the layout of colours in a paintbox was of greater importance to him than creating realistic images, referring to the paintbox as a 'chromatic keyboard'.

Over the next decades Klee produced many paintings that depicted colour in formations of carefully placed squares and rectangles, reminiscent of pressed watercolour blocks, colour charts in artists' guidebooks, or toy building blocks. His geometric compositions often appear like overlapping shapes and depict colour shading and gradation, or chromatic impressions such as evening light or sunsets. Further inspired by travels to North Africa, Klee became obsessed with colour, considering it the essence of painting: 'Colour and I are one. I am a painter,' he exclaimed in 1914, after having seen the light and colours of Tunisia. In the same year the First World War broke out, breaking up many recently founded artist movements and groups, including Der Blaue Reiter.

COLOUR FOR COLOUR'S SAKE – THE RADICAL EARLY TWENTIETH CENTURY 171

THE NOTEBOOKS

In 1925 Paul Klee published a 50-page volume of condensed versions of his lectures delivered during his early years at Bauhaus. This *Pädagogisches Skizzenbuch* (literally: *Pedagogical Sketchbook*, see above) was part of the small-format series Bauhausbücher, which ran between 1925–1930 and was edited and designed by Walter Gropius and László Moholy-Nagy. Apart from this and a couple of other modest volumes, Klee did not publish any of his writings or research on colour during his lifetime, but he left nearly 4000 pages of notes, sketches and diaries relating to Bauhaus principles (see overleaf) and his teaching between 1923 and 1931. These manuscripts were sent from Germany to Switzerland in a large trunk after Klee emigrated in December 1933, fleeing the Nazi regime. They are known as Klee's *Bildnerische Form- und Gestaltungslehre* (literally: *Pictorial doctrine on form and creation*) but more commonly referred to as *Paul Klee's Notebooks*, and survive in the archives of the Zentrum Paul Klee in Bern, Switzerland. Between the 1950s and 1970s parts of these notebooks were published by Jürg Spiller, but he received considerable criticism for taking much of Klee's work out of context. In 1970 a first facsimile and transcription of Klee's earliest lectures at Weimar were published by the Paul Klee Foundation, edited by Jürgen Glaesemer.

Klee's contributions to art and colour theory were considered so important that in 2012 the Paul Klee Zentrum in Bern digitised all the pages of his notebooks and made them available online, with transcriptions and annotations. These are highly personal sketches and notes, not edited or necessarily meant for immediate publication, but they give an unparalleled insight into Klee's thinking and particularly how closely he associated colour order with musical compositions. While some coloured sketches are relatively familiar geometric representations of colour order – overlapping squares, circles or triangles of colours representing colour mixtures – others convey more movement and rhythm. A number of them reveal how carefully the artist arranged colour squares in his most abstract compositions, assigning each hue a musical note, creating visual colour harmonies.

These facsimile manuscripts are an invaluable historical source and a prime example of knowledge and image capture in the digital age.

Above: Klee's *Pedagogical Sketchbook*, a coursebook produced for Bauhaus.

Right: One of several coloured pages of Klee's notebooks. Here he visualises the relationship between primary, secondary and tertiary colour mixtures in a diagram of overlapping triangles. On the right edge of the pages he added in pencil the hierarchical structure of these colours.

COLOUR FOR COLOUR'S SAKE – THE RADICAL EARLY TWENTIETH CENTURY

gleichen Teilen, und analog verhalten sich orange und violett wie Wirkungen zu ihren Ursachen GelbRot bezw. RotBlau. Wir sind also wohl berechtigt, den rechts erscheinenden Farben verschiedenen Rang beizumessen.

Darstellung

Die Geometrische des ganzen Geschehens wird uns dies mit noch knapperer Deutlichkeit zeigen.

Blau ... Blau	4 Blau + 0 Gelb	= Blau
	3 " + 1 "	= blaugrün
	2 " + 2 "	= grün
	1 " + 3 "	= grüngelb
Gelb ... Gelb	0 " + 4 "	= Gelb
	1 Rot + 3 "	= gelborange
	2 " + 2 "	= Orange
	3 " + 1 "	= orangerot
Rot ... Rot	4 " + 0 "	= Rot
	3 " + 1 Blau	= rotviolett
	2 " + 2 "	= violett
	1 " + 3 "	= violettblau
Blau ... Blau	0 " + 4 "	= Blau

fig.11

Jetzt springt der secundäre Charakter der drei Mischungen direct ins Auge. Ihre Einordnung in die primäre Blau= Gelb= und Rot bewegung kan klarer nicht zum Ausdruck kommen. Die Ursächlichkeit der drei Primäre

Bauhaus: Minimalist Colour in Art and Design

In 1921 Klee was invited to join the German art school Staatliches Bauhaus in Weimar, Germany, formed in 1919 by the modernist architect Walter Gropius and in the early years strongly informed by the Swiss painter and colour theorist Johannes Itten (see overleaf). Other significant members and teachers at the Bauhaus were Kandinsky, who joined in 1922, the sculptor Oskar Schlemmer, Oskar Kokoschka, Lyonel Feininger, László Moholy-Nagy, Theo van Doesburg and, later, Mies van der Rohe. Although the influence of Expressionism and even Art Nouveau was strong, Bauhaus style was radically minimalist, promoting clean lines, clarity, pure colours and strong materials. The overriding aim was to bring together the fine and applied arts, expressed in beautiful, simple and functional designs for all aspects of life, including kitchenware, furniture, toys and architecture. Like no other art and design movement, the Bauhaus school incorporated colour theory in teaching and practice, and Paul Klee was at the heart of this for ten years. He resigned from the Bauhaus, which had moved to Dessau and eventually Berlin, in 1931, to take up a position at the Düsseldorf Academy of Fine Art. In 1933 the Bauhaus was labelled 'un-German' by the Nazi party and the then Director Mies van der Rohe was forced to close it down. In the same year the Gestapo also removed Klee from his post in Düsseldorf, referring to his association with Bauhaus and labelling his art 'degenerate'.

Kandinsky, Itten and Klee all taught colour courses, giving it a prime role as a powerful tool in art and design, often alluding to its synaesthetic qualities. Kandinsky, who attempted to find a universal correspondence of primary colours and geometric shapes (see pages 158–161), asked his students to colour in shapes as part of a questionnaire. Although the results weren't uniform, the test highlights the correlation between form and colour as a key principle of Bauhaus design and art. The Bauhaus Cradle (opposite, bottom), originally designed in 1922 by Peter Keler, is a striking example of the use of geometry and colour in the design of everyday objects. It is constructed from red squares that form the sides, yellow triangles as head and foot of the cradle, held together by tubular, blue perfect circles that allow for a rocking motion. It comes as no surprise to learn that Keler was a student of Kandinsky.

In 1923 one of Itten's students, Alma Siedhoff-Buscher, designed a set of toy building blocks for a children's room of a model Bauhaus building in Weimar. *Bauspiel: Ein Schiff* (right, top) is just one of many examples of the clean lines, geometric shapes, robust materials and the use of strong primary and secondary colours in Bauhaus designs. These and other colourful building blocks were marketed for both children and adults, encouraging them to order colour into either abstract three-dimensional compositions or recognisable structures, such as ships or bridges. Like the trichromatic cradle and many other functional objects, Siedhoff-Buscher's set of building blocks remains in production today.

Above: *Bauspiel: Ein Schiff* is a set of toy blocks designed in classic Bauhaus colour and shape.

Right: The Bauhaus Cradle from 1922 introduces the clean lines and pure colours to a baby's cot.

COLOUR FOR COLOUR'S SAKE – THE RADICAL EARLY TWENTIETH CENTURY

The Art of Colour: Theory and Phenomenon

Opposite: Itten proposed a colour globe as the ideal form for visualising colour. Elevations of the globe can be seen at the bottom of the page, while its opened-out form presents as a 12-pointed star.

Overleaf: In this spread from the chapter on the 'Theory of Colour Expression' in *The Art of Color* Itten uses examples inspired by the four seasons to demonstrate complex harmonies in colour palettes exemplifying different qualities; for example the 'luminous colours' of spring (fig. 146); yellow and yellow-green with contrasting pinks and blues to 'amplify and enrich the chord'. Winter (fig. 149), by contrast, typifies 'passivity in nature' and 'require[s] colours connoting withdrawal'.

Like Paul Klee, Johannes Itten was a Swiss-German painter who taught at the Bauhaus school – only relatively briefly, but during the experimental first years from 1919 to 1923. Invited by the school's founder Walter Gropius, who initially gave him a completely free hand, Itten developed and delivered the 'Basic Course', in which students were given a chance to work in a number of different materials and attend short lectures on art theory, including colour, as well as on general subjects from everyday life.

Itten famously started his lessons with relaxation and breathing exercises, replacing the traditional morning prayer, with the aim of concentrating the students' thoughts on the day's subject. Ideas of rhythm, contrast and composition were compared and applied to breathing patterns and physical movement, a method that caused initial bafflement among some students, but helped many to relax and focus. Despite introducing radical and experimental teaching methods, Itten was most strongly inspired by the seemingly more traditional and analytical approach of one of his own teachers, Adolf Hölzel, who in turn had been influenced by Goethe's writings on colour. According to Itten, Hölzel had put much emphasis in his lectures on meticulously analysing the line and colour composition of Old Master paintings.

Itten's colour theory was based on a twelve-part colour wheel developed from three primaries (yellow, red and blue) and three secondaries (green, orange and violet). He further formulated seven contrast effects of colours: (1) pure colour (hue), (2) light-dark, (3) cold-warm, (4) complementary, (5) simultaneous, (6) quality (saturation) and (7) quantity. Itten wished to 'liberate the study of colour harmonies from associations with form' and – perhaps inspired by Klee – considered the chess board the most suitable pattern for colour studies (overleaf). In an attempt to provide 'a clear and complete map of the world in colour' he developed his colour wheel into a colour sphere, if only in two-dimensional form (opposite, bottom). His twelve-pointed colour star (opposite, top; Itten himself referred to it as both a star and a sphere) is a colour diagram that can be projected on to a three-dimensional globe, with a graded tonality of the twelve colours – arranged in pure form around the equator – from light (white) to dark (black), as proposed by other colour theorists such as Runge and Munsell before him (see page 144).

Itten wished to 'liberate the study of colour harmonies from associations with form'

Itten left the Bauhaus after an argument with Gropius about his teaching methodology in 1923 and opened his own art school in Berlin in 1926. Like the Bauhaus school Itten's art college came under pressure from the Nazis and he felt forced to dissolve it in 1934. In 1938, refusing to adopt German nationality, he emigrated to Switzerland.

The Second World War and its immediate aftermath caused a long gap in the publication of significant writings on colour by the wider Bauhaus circle, but in 1961 Itten triumphed with an ambitious and state-of-the-art book on colour that became an immediate classic. *Kunst der Farbe* (*The Art of Color*) was published simultaneously in German and in an English translation by Ernst van Haagen. It was immediately made available in America where it was influential in the field of abstract colour and other art movements. Within ten years it was translated into French, Serbo-Croatian, Italian and Japanese. The book's subtitle *Subjektives Erleben und objektives Erkennen als Wege zur Kunst* (*The subjective experience and objective rationale of color*) reflects both Itten's interest in psychoanalysis and his desire to provide a reliable instructive colour system for general use in art and design.

COLOUR FOR COLOUR'S SAKE – THE RADICAL EARLY TWENTIETH CENTURY

THEORY OF COLOR EXPRESSION

The optical, electromagnetic and chemical processes initiated in the eye and brain are frequently paralleled by processes in the psychological realm. Such reverberations of the experience of color may be propagated to the inmost centers, thereby affecting principal areas of mental and emotional experience. Goethe spoke of the ethico-aesthetic activity of colors. By careful analysis, I shall try to elucidate this topic, so important to the color artist.

I recall the following anecdote:

A businessman was entertaining a party of ladies and gentlemen at dinner. The arriving guests were greeted by delicious smells issuing from the kitchen, and all were eagerly anticipating the meal. As the happy company assembled about the table, laden with good things, the host flooded the apartment with red light. The meat looked rare and appetizing enough, but the spinach turned black and the potatoes were bright red. Before the guests had recovered from their astonishment, the red light changed to blue, the roast assumed an aspect of putrefaction and the potatoes looked moldy. All the diners lost their appetite at once; but when the yellow light was turned on, transforming the claret into castor oil and the company into living cadavers, some of the more delicate ladies hastily rose and left the room. No one could think of eating, though all present knew it was only a change in the color of the lighting. The host laughingly turned the white lights on again, and soon the good spirits of the gathering were restored. Who can doubt that colors exert profound influences upon us, whether we are aware of them or not?

The deep blue of the sea and distant mountains enchants us; the same blue as an interior seems uncanny, lifeless, and terrifying. Blue reflections on the skin render it pale, as if moribund. In the dark of night, a blue neon light is attractive, like blue on black, and in conjunction with red and yellow lights it lends a cheerful, lively tone. A blue sun-filled sky has an active and enlivening effect, whereas the mood of the blue moonlit sky is passive and evokes subtle nostalgias.

Redness in the face denotes wrath or fever; a blue, green or yellow complexion, sickness, though there is nothing sickly about the pure colors. A red sky threatens bad weather; a blue, green or yellow sky promises fair weather.

On the basis of these experiences of nature, it would seem all but impossible to formulate simple and true propositions about the expressive content of colors.

Yellow shadows, violet light, blue-green fire, red-orange ice, are effects in apparent contradiction with experience, and give an other-worldly expression. Only those deeply responsive can experience the tonal values of single or simultaneous colors without reference to objects. Musical experience is denied to those with no ear for music.

The example of the four seasons, Figs. 146 to 149, shows that color sensation and experience have objective correlatives, even though each individual sees, feels and evaluates color in a very personal way. I have often maintained that the judgment "pleasing-displeasing" can be no valid criterion of true and correct coloration. A serviceable yardstick is obtained only if we base each judgment on the relation and relative position of each color with respect to the adjacent color and the totality of colors. Stated in terms of the four seasons, this means that for each season we are to find those colors, those points on and in the color sphere, that distinctly belong to the expression of that season in their relation to the whole universe of colors.

The youthful, light, radiant generation of nature in Spring is expressed by luminous colors; Fig. 146. Yellow is the color nearest to white light, and yellow-green is its intensification. Light pink and light blue tones amplify and enrich the chord. Yellow, pink and lilac are often seen in the buds of plants.

The colors for Autumn contrast most sharply with those of Spring. In Autumn, the green of vegetation dies out, to be broken down and decomposed into dull brown and violet; Fig. 148.

The promise of Spring is fulfilled in the maturity of Summer.

Nature in Summer, thrust materially outward into a maximum luxuriance of form and color, attains extreme density and a vividly plastic fullness of powers. Warm, saturated, active colors, to be found at their peak in only one particular region of the color sphere, offer themselves for the expression of Summer; Fig. 147. For contrast with and amplification of these principal colors, their complements will of course also be required.

To represent Winter, typifying passivity in nature by a contracting, inward movement of the forces of earth, we require colors connoting withdrawal, cold and centripetal radiance, transparency, rarefaction; Fig. 149.

Above & opposite: In about 1949, after Albers had settled in Newhaven, Connecticut, he began exploring the relationship between colours and colour and space in a series of almost 2,000 paintings referred to as 'Homage to the Square'. This is an example of Albers experimenting with shades of green. A tin box of green paints used by him survives in the archives of the Josef and Anni Albers Foundation.

Kunst der Farbe was an impressive vehicle for Itten's modern colour theory and its application in art. Produced in a large square format (29 x 31 cm), the 155-page volume is elegantly bound in pale grey cloth, using Bauhaus-informed minimalist typography. Most importantly, it contains no fewer than 174 photographic tipped-in plates with colour diagrams and related images, and an additional 28 colour plates of Old Master paintings (here his teacher Hölzel's influence is obvious) and works by modern artists, such as Piet Mondrian, Henri Matisse and, of course, Klee. Among the images are Itten's well-known twelve-part colour circle, the colour sphere (star), plates illustrating simultaneous contrast, colour composition, mixing and the use of colour as an expressive tool (see pages 176–177). The greatest of care was clearly taken in the reproduction and printing of the plates and the book must have been an ambitious publishing project in its time. In his acknowledgements Itten mentions the 'painstaking attention to color fidelity' that was paid by the design company Graphische Anstalt E. Wartelsteiner, who produced most of the illustrations. In 1973 an improved edition was printed, utilising further advances in colour printing.

Itten's *Art of Color* had a strong impact on the art world and modern colour theory, and his lavish volume was soon after followed by smaller publications documenting his Bauhaus teaching and methodology. Other important publications on colour appeared in the wake of Itten's book and heralded a new era of ambitious book design. Among them was one by Itten's former student, the German artist, colour researcher and teacher Josef Albers who, after the closure of Bauhaus, had emigrated to America, where he taught art, design and colour at various institutions, including Yale University.

Albers was less interested in scientific colour theory than the practical and phenomenal aspects of the use and combination of colour, especially in 'hard-edge' abstract art. For nearly 30 years he experimented both as an artist and a teacher with the ways colours appear, how they influence each other, and how the human eye and brain perceive them. It is not surprising that the publication that made him famous, *Interaction of Color*, was essentially a beautifully executed, didactic and inspiring book of optical exercises.

It was Yale University Press who in 1963 first published Albers's hugely popular book in a limited edition with 150 silkscreen-printed plates, showing predominantly Albers's distinctive overlapping colour squares and rectangles. This elegant and highly instructive book, in which the author decrees that colour is a more important pictorial element than form, was eventually published in a pocket-format paperback in 1971 and has never been out of print since. In 2009 Yale reproduced the original silk-screen edition in a lavish new edition and in 2013 made it available in digital interactive form as a mobile app.

COLOUR FOR COLOUR'S SAKE – THE RADICAL EARLY TWENTIETH CENTURY

COLOUR FOR COLOUR'S SAKE – THE RADICAL EARLY TWENTIETH CENTURY   181

Psychological Colour for the Modern Home

Just after the First World War, the aesthetic ideals of clarity, functionality, good design and sparing use of ornament as advocated by the Bauhaus Group and other Modernist movements and styles gave rise to the use of primary colours and bolder schemes in interior decoration, furniture and household objects. Illustrated books on how to use colour in your home followed a book that was less concerned with avant-garde style and architecture and treated all colours and style of buildings and interiors equally. It is illustrated with black-and-white photographs and a number of coloured plates with images after photographs where considerable retouching is noticeable. The interiors shown are not radical modern schemes but a range of rooms from buildings of all ages. The chapters deal with eleven colours and their uses individually, followed by additional chapters on colour contrast, practical issues, as well as an unusual one that deals with the dislike of colours, in which Ionides discusses why and how certain colours go temporarily out of fashion ('Disrepute of colours').

The author weaves in psychological notions, for example how we respond emotionally to colour and express ourselves through colour

Above & opposite: The frontispiece to Basil Ionides' *Colour and Interior Decoration* (above) features a traditional wood-panelled bedroom, marking its disregard for trends and applying its theories to rooms and buildings of any description. Here, 'a bedroom with brown walls enlivened by bright colour'. The room featured on the frontispiece to John Gloag's *Colour & Comfort* (opposite), on the other hand, is the height of interior fashion.

quickly and became hugely popular, and photography was now being used widely to illustrate print media, although colour reproduction of photographs was still in its infancy and considerably more expensive than older methods such as lithography. In 1924 John Gloag wrote about the 'power of colour' and suggested economical and effective ways of making the most of this power in twentieth-century houses. Finding a balance between colour and form, with the aim of creating comfortable interiors, is the main theme in his book *Colour & Comfort* (opposite). It is illustrated with line drawings throughout, but the frontispiece shows an open plan sitting and dining room in which blues, greens and yellows dominate. The floor is shiny and the lines are geometric and clean – a truly modern interior.

Just two years later, the architect Basil Ionides published *Colour and Interior Decoration* (above),

In addition to his focus on practical advice and design guidelines, the author weaves in psychological notions, for example how we respond emotionally to colour and express ourselves through colour choices in interiors:

The psychology of colour effect is held to influence many people and to show character greatly. Most people wish to express their personality in their rooms, and most people do this with colour. Blues in deeper tones are said to be restful and to tend to contemplation and philosophy. It is a peaceful colour. Green having blue in it and also yellow, which is a cheerful colour, is happy and is affected by those whose life is contented. Mauve belongs to the weak, morbid, and discontented. Pink is apt to be cruel as it has red rays in it, and red is essentially a cruel colour.

The book became a best-seller and was followed in 1934 by the also successful *Colour in Everyday Rooms*.

A Sitting Room and Dining Room

Above right: A colour chart from Patmore's 1933 *Colour Schemes for the Modern Home* resembles a gas flame, burning from deep red through orange, yellow and green, to a deep blue.

Opposite: Patmore's book is an early example of photographic illustrations of interiors printed in full colour. The plates show a variety of rooms, both modern and traditional, both multicoloured and monochromatic.

In 1933, the young and aspiring British writer Derek Coventry Patmore published a stylish book on contemporary interior design entitled *Colour Schemes for the Modern Home*. Patmore came from an intellectual family that moved in artistic circles, but his father had to file for bankruptcy in the 1920s and his parents split up soon after. Patmore spent some of the 1920s in New York, immersing himself in the design scene and writing for *Vogue* and *House and Garden*. Patmore's book is unusual for a 1930s publication on interior design because he discusses not just colour as used in interiors but also colour theory and psychology. In the 30 pages of text preceding the 24 photographic tipped-in colour plates showing actual contemporary interiors, Patmore writes at considerable length about the effects of colour on mood. He begins by explaining that the scientific examination of colour is a relatively recent subject and places Isaac Newton at the beginning of colour studies, going on to mention several other theorists including Johann Heinrich Lambert, Goethe and Ostwald. Subscribing to the material view of colour, he even includes a plate with a colour chart of nine varieties of colours derived from the primaries red, yellow and blue, demonstrating how the colours mix (above).

However, Patmore's intention was not to add another textbook on colour or colour theory. His aim was to provide suggestions as to how colour can be usefully applied in interiors. 'How many of us stop to analyse our feelings and reactions to colours?' he asks. 'Yet modern science tells us that the colours we live with can make us either depressed or happy. A room may be cheerful, restful, or thoroughly depressing by reason of the shades of colour used for its decoration.'

Patmore continued with a list of the possible psychological associations (both positive and negative) of the main colours yellow, red, blue, dark blue, green and black, connected with their applications. Blue, for example, he explains, 'is associated in our minds with peace but it can also suggest coldness. Dark blue, however, used sparingly, such as on a ceiling in a bedroom, will be found very soothing'.

The rooms shown in Patmore's photographic illustrations are joyfully modern, and the plates are all in colour. Many of the rooms have one dominant colour or combine a few strong, complementary colours. There is, for example, an all-white living room (opposite, top left), designed by Syrie Maugham, and an apple-green dining room (opposite, bottom right) accented with silver and chrome. A room designed by the Bloomsbury Group artists Duncan Grant and Vanessa Bell combines yellows and whites with brown and blues (opposite, top right). Most of the furnishings are contemporary but occasionally antique furniture is contrasted with brightly coloured walls and twentieth-century artwork, as for example in a room by John Armstrong, where 'a colour scheme of sky blue, burnt sienna and golden yellow' (opposite, bottom left) forms the background for dark wood Chippendale chairs.

184 COLOUR FOR COLOUR'S SAKE – THE RADICAL EARLY TWENTIETH CENTURY

COLOUR FOR COLOUR'S SAKE – THE RADICAL EARLY TWENTIETH CENTURY

Practical and Beautiful: The Art of Colour Printing

Thomas E. Griffits was a much-respected printer and writer who worked for many years for the colour printing companies Vincent Brooks Day & Son and The Baynard Press, both operating in London. He specialized in lithographic reproduction of early twentieth-century works of art and wrote a number of popular handbooks on the art and technique of lithographic printing, inspiring many contemporary artists and designers.

Lithography had been invented in 1796 by the German Alois Senefelder. It involved drawing on a close grain and absorbent stone with a greasy paint or ink before etching its surface slightly with a weak acid solution, dampening the stone and then applying ink to it with a roller. Unlike other printing methods it was 'planographic', meaning the print surface is flat, and relied on the base of water and grease not mixing. The resulting images were softer and grainier than those from etchings or engravings, giving the appearance of a colour wash or a chalk drawing. Lithographic printing was championed in Britain by the publisher Rudolph Ackermann in the early nineteenth century. He not only published a translation of Senefelder's treatise on this new and exciting printing method (*A Complete Course of Lithography*, from 1819), but also set up a lithography press in London and began incorporating lithographic illustrations into several of his popular magazines and other publications. By the late nineteenth century, lithography had developed from pure line drawing to a three- or four-colour printing process, creating coloured images by overlaying transparent printing ink in cyan, magenta, yellow and black. Both early drawn lithography and the later technique of overlay printing would prove highly useful for colour illustration and the reproduction of artwork.

With *The Technique of Colour Printing by Lithography: A Concise Manual of Drawn Lithography* Griffits's intention was to provide a practical and easy-to-use reference book for artists using or intending to use the lithographic method. First published by Faber and Faber in 1940 and reissued in 1944, it is an impressive example of how a beautiful and relatively

Opposite: Griffits's beautiful and inventive *The Technique of Colour Printing*, first published in 1940.

COLOUR FOR COLOUR'S SAKE – THE RADICAL EARLY TWENTIETH CENTURY

COLOUR FOR COLOUR'S SAKE – THE RADICAL EARLY TWENTIETH CENTURY

complex book on colour could be produced during the war years. The format of the book is small (21 x 14 cm) and the paper – typical for many books published during or just after the Second World War – is greyish and thin. Despite these restrictions the book is highly appealing. The simple green-and-black cloth boards are subtly decorated in imitation of the variety of textures and looks achieved through lithographic printing.

CUT-OUTS AND FOLD-OUTS

Griffits's book contains many drawings of printing tools and techniques, and a number of coloured plates illustrating the various stages of the printing process. A fold-out chart on stiffer paper shows a range of strengths of colours produced in overprinting (see previous page and above), as well as a plate that illustrates the effect of coloured or textured paper. Most interesting though, are the 'colour stops' included in the form of loose bookmarks and templates with cut-out windows that can be laid over plates of colour charts (above). They allow the reader to isolate certain colours and experiment with colour combinations. One can imagine how these bookmarks would be useful for comparing the appearance of a colour both in combination with others and on its own. Griffits was not the first to use overlay templates with cut-out areas that help isolate colours: a similar technique was used by Moses Harris and his colour charts in *Natural System of Colours* in the 1770s (see pages 26–29), and in the early twentieth century Wilhelm Ostwald had included a small colour stop in the form of a bookmark on a ribbon in his colour manuals (see pages 166–169). Griffits's colour stops are thin and fragile but, with relatively simple means, he and his publisher managed to produce a highly useful manual on colour printing in the 1940s. In the introduction Frank Pick noted that this book was 'a piece of impersonal biography, for it summarises and explains the practice of lithography as Mr. Griffits has known and elaborated it over nearly forty years, and stands as a record of his business life.'

Above & opposite: Griffits's book is replete with fold-out plates, and cut-out bookmarks and 'colour stops'. Readers could place the colour stops over various parts of the diagrams to isolate colours, the better to analyse their effects and interactions.

COLOUR FOR COLOUR'S SAKE – THE RADICAL EARLY TWENTIETH CENTURY

COMPARISON OF THE REFLECTION OF COLOURS

Plate 2

A Colour Dictionary: The Villalobos *Colour Atlas*

One of the most extensive twentieth-century colour identification systems in print culture was produced in 1947 by the Argentinian artist Cándido Villalobos-Domínguez and his architect son Julio Villalobos. Their *Atlas de los Colores/Colour Atlas* was published in a bilingual Spanish/English edition in Buenos Aires, Argentina. It aimed to help printers, artists, scientists and designers identify colours in an era when mechanical tools for measuring colour and light intensity (spectrophotometers) were still considered an unrealistic option for many designers. The large (22 x 32 cm), sturdy and attractively designed book was going to be the affordable alternative, and it is clear that the authors and publishers were targeting a wide international audience.

A 'Chromatic Hexagon', similar to many other twelve-part colour wheels, based on six spectral colours (here named Yellow, Green, Turquoise, Ultramarine, Magenta and Scarlet) forms a reference image for the Villalobos system and is followed by a brief introductory text section. The other 38 pages contain 7279 glossy printed colour chips, each measuring 1 x 1 cm, arranged

COLOUR FOR COLOUR'S SAKE – THE RADICAL EARLY TWENTIETH CENTURY

Above left & above right:
Two plates of colour chips from the 1947 *Colour Atlas*, showing shades of green (opposite) and ruby (above).

in colour groups and pasted on to the plates. Each of the colour chips has a tiny off-centre hole, which allows users to see through to other pages and compare the tints with others. The plates are arranged in the style of a dictionary, with a thumbnail colour index along the bottom edge of the print block. They can also be removed, as they are not glue-bound but held together in ring-binder style.

The organisation of the *Colour Atlas* follows the CIELAB system – a colour space measuring system of all colours visible to the human eye that was developed by the Commission internationale de l'éclairage (International Commission on Illumination), founded in 1913 – but it also shows similarities to Munsell's system (see pages 140–145). The *Atlas* was an ambitious attempt to produce in print a comprehensive system of colour mixtures. Intended as a tool, it was soon superseded by new technology, but it is an aesthetically pleasing and highly tactile book on colour that was designed for practical use and extensive physical handling.

COLOUR FOR COLOUR'S SAKE – THE RADICAL EARLY TWENTIETH CENTURY

Colour into the Future: The Wheels Keep On Spinning

After a dark and difficult period in print culture during and immediately after the Second World War, popular magazines and paint manuals from the late 1940s onwards encouraged readers to opt for a daring use of colour in order to mark a new beginning and to boost morale. In the 1950s and '60s consumers once again began to fully embrace colour in fashion, art and architecture. Books, magazines, advertising material and ephemera promoting colour, paints and design schemes were produced in large quantities.

Many publications on colour in the immediate post-war years were printed on relatively low-quality paper, but despite these material restrictions the passion for colour and the desire to push book design and colour illustration forward is evident. Indeed, many of the most stunning books on colour by teachers and artists from the Bauhaus circle, as seen in the previous chapter, were actually published in the 1960s and '70s, when photographic colour printing had developed much further and had almost entirely replaced hand-colouring and metal-plate or woodblock printing. However, as we see in examples such as the contemporary paint sample cards of Patrick Baty's Papers and Paints company, in certain areas the meticulous and reliable technique of representing colours and paints as real paint samples prevails. The later twentieth century saw the advent of digital printing in colour, which is now the standard form of book illustration.

From the beginning of the twentieth century, CMYK (a subtractive colour model in which all colours can be made out of four pigments: cyan, magenta, yellow and black) was understood as the basis of colour printing. By the middle of the century this was standardised, when the printing company M & J Levine Advertising hired a chemist, Lawrence Herbert, in 1956, to systematise their colour production. In 1962, Herbert bought the company and renamed it Pantone. The result of his efforts was a colour matching system, intended to make it possible for designers to identify and discuss colours accurately and for manufacturers to reproduce a colour exactly, no matter what equipment they used. Similar attempts at colour standardisation had been made before, but this was the most successful. Today Pantone and its proprietary Pantone Matching System (PMS) is an industry standard across the globe.

In the 1950s and '60s, consumers once again began to embrace colour in fashion, art and architecture

At the same time as companies like Pantone were applying standards, other industries were employing a more experimental use of colour, for example in the Brutalist architecture of the 1950s and '60s. One of the areas this is most interesting to observe is newly built and restored religious buildings as in Sir Basil Spence's designs. Here, the symbolic use of coloured glass was both tapping into ancient traditions and reflecting new ideas such as deliberately juxtaposing contrasting building materials or reinterpreting colour order in a religious context.

The renowned Centre Georges Pompidou in Paris, built in the 1970s, meanwhile, combines utility with decoration in its application of colour. The building's unique design places all functional structures outside, maximising the space inside. Adopting a tetrachromatic system, the architects made colour a key part of their design, assigning each function a colour; for example, pipes for circulating air are coloured blue, electrical cables are encased in yellow pipes, water pipes are green and lifts and escalators are coloured red.

Left: Basil Spence's design for the Meeting House Chapel, completed in 1966, references traditional stained glass windows, a feature of church architecture since the seventh century, while also embracing new ideas about colour by using it in an abstract way.

While there is a long tradition of painters depicting themselves with their palettes and other painters' tools, in the twentieth and twenty-first centuries many artists made colour order and colour theory in particular a theme in their art, with varying degrees of overt references to specific writings on colour. We saw how in the early twentieth century many artists embraced colour as a powerful expressive tool. They explored the symbolic and spiritual connotations of colour, giving it more compositional importance than it had ever before enjoyed. Colour retained this importance into the twenty-first century, but here, in contrast with the meaning-laden function of colour of previous decades, Modernist movements in America and Europe utilised colour as an abstract absolute, often devoid of any representative quality. By the mid-twentieth century, artists such as Barnett Newman, Mark Rothko, Bridget Riley, Gerhard Richter and countless others were making artworks that seemed to celebrate colour, just for colour's sake. They often worked (and some still do) on a monumental scale, making full use of the visual power of pure colour without figurative representation, but their work is grounded in theories of colour harmony developed decades or even centuries earlier. Rothko, for example, is famous for his highly abstract works that place two or three colours, or shades of a colour, over each other in simple rectangular forms. The viewer is invited to consider the qualities of the colours in themselves and in combination with each other; the longer one stares, the more expansive the colour seems to become, offering more of itself up to be noticed.

One artist for whom colour was a main concern was Yves Klein, whose particular obsession was with the colour blue. Until the invention of Prussian blue in the eighteenth century, the best blue pigment (ultramarine) was prohibitively expensive, and its use was almost entirely limited to the depiction of holy, religious subjects, such as the Virgin Mary. As we saw with the example of Kandinsky (see page 162–165), blue retained its associations with spirituality into the twentieth cenutury. Until his death in 1962, Klein, too, was interested in precisely this aspect of his chosen colour, which expressed it through monochrome paintings made with 'IKB' or International Klein Blue a pigment based on ultramarine that he himself had invented, with the help of a modern-day 'colourman', the Parisian paint supplier Edouard Adam. The key to this bluest of blues was the binder Rhodopas that allowed the ultramarine to retain more of its intensity than traditional binders.

The pursuit of the purest and most stable of colours has remained a theme for artists since humans began painting, but it certainly seems to have become a theme in the later twentieth and twenty-first centuries. British sculptor and painter Anish Kapoor, for example, frequently worked with bright, primary colours, but in 2014 he made himself somewhat unpopular in the artworld by obtaining an exclusive license to work with Vantablack – the 'blackest black'. In response, Kapoor's fellow artist Stuart Semple created 'the world's pinkest pink', a pigment he made available to all artists except Kapoor, whom he banned from using it.

Left: Mark Rothko's *Light Red Over Black* (1957) invites the viewer to meditate on the colours seen on the canvas.

Modernist movements in America and Europe utilised colour as an abstract absolute

The examples of Klein, Kapoor and Semple show how important material colour remains for artists; however, new technologies have always played a part in determining the kinds of works that will be made in a particular time. In the latter twentieth century through to the present day, this has often meant incorporating electronics and digital technologies into artworks, allowing artists to explore immaterial colour as never before. David Batchelor is just one example of an artist using technological developments to represent immaterial through video installations and coloured lights.

In recent years, many graphic designers and conceptual artists have been responding to traditional and new ideas and concepts of colour, with some of them literally putting a new spin on colour wheels. The continued fascination with colour and its abstract nature and beauty remains a popular and dominant theme in many domains of our culture. This book can provide only a very small and subjective selection of recent artistic interpretations of colour order and colour systems, but it will hopefully give a taste of the role concepts of colour still play in the creative process.

196 COLOUR INTO THE FUTURE – THE WHEELS KEEP ON SPINNING

Simple and Pictorial: A Children's Guide to Printing

Left: The cover of Harold Curwen's *Printing*, an introductory title aimed at children. The cover manages to fit many elements of the print trade into its design, including a letterpress of the title, backwards, of course.

This booklet, straightforwardly titled *Printing* (1948), was the 70th title in Penguin's Puffin Picture Book series. This series was aimed at young readers between the ages of seven and fourteen and covered a wide range of topics, with a strong focus on natural history and technology. Produced at the beginning of the Second World War, the first three volumes were highly topical: *War on Land*, *War at Sea* and *War in the Air* (all published in 1940). The series was marked by the clarity, figurative detail and strong colours we often associate with children's books of the mid-twentieth century. It ran to a total of 120 volumes until 1965, with the post-war volumes being noticeably more colourful. The series' aim was to be both educational and entertaining.

This particular volume was written by none other than Harold Curwen, who was running the famous Curwen Press, founded by his father, John Curwen, in 1863. Under Harold, the press became especially known for high-quality and stylish typography, book designs and lithographic printing. Fittingly, this Puffin volume was itself lithographed by the Curwen Press. The booklet is illustrated in detailed and colourful style by Jack Brough. His cover design shows various tools of the printing trade, and includes an image of the three primary, overlapping print colours on the cover, which form secondaries and combine into a black centre, much like the earliest published colour wheels for artists. This colour diagram is a simple, abstract and bold feature placed like a final seal on a cover design that is wonderfully literal and direct.

POPPY RED

16

EQUIVALENT TO
BRITISH COLOUR COUNCIL
RIDGWAY
REPERTOIRE
OSTWALD

Poppy B.C.C. 97
Scarlet 5
Rouge Grenadier 82/1
XIV 6 pa

History:
General representation of the wild corn Poppy, as used by the textile and paint trades for over 200 years.

Foreign Synonyms:

Dutch: Papaverrood
French: Rouge Coquelicot
German: Mohnrot
Italian: Rosso di Papavero
Latin: Papaverinus
Spanish: Punzón

Horticultural Examples:

16/3

16/2

16/1 *Fuchsia serratifolia* (petals)
Macleania insignis

16 *Papaver orientale*
Streptosolen Jamesonii
Solanum Capsicastrum (fruit)

16/3

16/2

16/1

16

Robert Francis Wilson and the Post-War Workspace

In 1931 Robert Francis Wilson, a British designer and dedicated researcher, founded the British Colour Council. Over the course of the next twenty years, this organisation would produce colour charts and reference codes for various industries. Wilson himself produced several colour charts and wheels in this period, perhaps most importantly, the first volume of a horticultural colour chart in 1938, in collaboration with the Royal Horticultural Society. The eponymous *Wilson Colour Chart* (left) was a collection of 100 individual plates with printed colour samples, hole-punched to allow users to remove plates as they needed. Each colour was reproduced in four degrees of saturation and the accompanying text was factual, precise and highly informative, including the equivalent of the colour in other colour systems, the colour name in six foreign languages and a very brief history of each colour. Three years later, Volume Two, comprising a further 100 plates, was published. A later reissue contained the plates loose in a folder.

The aim of the *Wilson Colour Chart* was to produce a reliable and international standard of colours; a standard to be measured in flowers, so to speak, but for use far beyond the realm of horticulture:

> *There will thus be but one colour name recognised for each hue in the textile and all colour-using industries as well as by artists' colourmen. While therefore, the colours chosen and names used have been selected primarily for the purposes of horticulture, the Royal Horticultural Society Colour Chart will also have a use and value far outside its horticultural scope.*

Left: Wilson's colour chart from 1938 aimed to provide a useful standard and reference chart, comprising 100 plates in the first volume and translating each colour given into its equivalent in different languages and colour systems.

But Wilson also had a great interest in the psychological impact of colour. His 1953 publication *Colour and Light at Work* focusses on how we respond to colour in our immediate environment and offers a fascinating insight into concerns about working conditions in the post-war years. Wilson comments in his preface that he is grateful 'to live at a time when colour and light are recognised as partners in helping to combat sickness, improving working conditions for millions of people, and making their work safer and more enjoyable'. The small-format book was illustrated with charts and diagrams supporting Wilson's arguments for the careful and deliberate colouring and lighting of both workspaces and the machines themselves.

In the book's twelve coloured plates, Wilson included illustrations of abstract colour theory, such as 'juxtaposition', which deals with the effects that colours have on each other, in various combinations.

Six of the plates, however, show industrial working spaces and machinery, visually making a case for using colour as both a psychological and a safety tool. Plate 12, for example (opposite), addresses depression caused by working conditions, drawing comparisons with a lack of sunlight: 'Successive days of dull grey skies promote a feeling of depression; drab, untidy, dreary workrooms have the same effect. What a difference in mental outlook when the sky is bright with sunshine, what a change of heart to work in rooms made cheerful with colour.'

This lesser-known book of Wilson's is a mid-twentieth-century expression of thoughts on the psychological and emotional aspect of colour first voiced by Johann Wolfgang von Goethe, Thomas Hope, Humphry Repton and others 150 years earlier.

This page: Three of Wilson's diagrams illustrating his colour theory, including his chromatic circle showing 'the full intensity' of different pigments (top left), one of his Juxtaposition plates (top right), and the 'after-image' effect (left).

Right: A more figurative plate explains 'The Value of Colour in Industry' comparing a drab workroom to overcast skies.

PLATE 12. THE VALUE OF COLOUR IN INDUSTRY.

Successive days of dull grey skies promote a feeling of depression; drab, untidy, dreary workrooms have the same effect. What a difference in mental outlook when the sky is bright with sunshine, what a change of heart to work in rooms made cheerful with colour.

Accent on Colour: A Bold New Palette

Above, left & right: The *Accent on Colour* supplement in *Homes and Gardens* advertised the modern palette to all shapes and sizes of household.

Opposite: An advert for the 'Spectro-Matic Colour Dispenser', promising an 'infinitely varied choice of paint colours'. The colours are shown against a 'contrasting carpet shade', but it's not clear whether these were recommended combinations for decoration.

The desire and, indeed, the need in the post-war years to create interiors with brighter and stronger colours reached its climax in the 1960s. A distinct sense of wanting to make a fresh start and to leave the dark, difficult and lean period of the war behind is apparent in many areas of culture and industry. It was an age of joyful and experimental consumerism, manufacturing and advertising, and colour played a major role in expressing this newfound zest for life. Ephemera such as the *Homes and Gardens* gift booklet titled *Accent on Colour* (above), produced in association with, and essentially an advert for, the paint manufacturer Walter Carson & Sons Ltd. in 1960, were mass-produced and became common. Here, modern bungalows are pictured alongside Georgian terraces, and suggested colour schemes are vibrant and shimmery. The booklet suggests, for example, 'an orange-painted ceiling to add invigorating warmth to pale silvery walls. Lay deep blue linoleum on the floor and paint a matching blue door – both practical and smart'. Machines, so Walter Carson & Sons Ltd. informs us, will help you mix the shade you desire and match it with others: Carson's 'Spectro-Matic Colour Dispenser' gives you the option to choose from a range of displayed colours and produce them immediately. The 'hazards of home decorating' have been abolished.

SPECTRO-MATIC COLOUR DISPENSER

The Spectro-matic colour dispensing machine produces an infinitely varied choice of paint colours in any Ultralux finish. Five colours are shown here each in two tones with a contrasting carpet shade. See page 2.

COLOUR INTO THE FUTURE – THE WHEELS KEEP ON SPINNING

'This is Color Surprise': Popular Art Manuals in 1950s and '60s America

Above left: The covers of Foster's manuals were designed to catch the eyes of browsing customers. In this example he tried to convey the materiality and three-dimensionality of paint by using colour photography.

Above right: Foster's color chart is full of information. Incorporating both the shape of a wheel and a star, his diagram succinctly explains material colour mixing. Further illustrations explore concepts such as cold/warm colours, and colour harmonies.

Opposite: In 'This is Color Surprise', Foster shows how to 'create the illusion of light and shadow of a color'.

In the second half of the twentieth century, newspapers, magazines and periodicals became larger in format and more lavishly illustrated, with most publications moving towards colour illustration. Amateur painting manuals published in the 1950s and 1960s reflected new trends in fashion and popular culture and many, especially American examples, are particularly vibrant, bold and experimental in their use of colour and design.

In the 1950s the American amateur artist and businessman Walter T. Foster began self-publishing oversized (35 x 26 cm) art manuals in a magazine style with little text but many large and colourful images. Foster had founded Walter Foster Publishing in 1922 and was working from his home in California, with complete control over his publications. At first he authored, illustrated, printed and packaged every manual himself, aiming to create affordable, exciting and modern-looking art manuals. The manuals were displayed in specially designed metal racks, allowing the customer to see the striking covers. Foster's manuals were hugely successful and over time he started employing other artists and authors to work on specific subjects, publishing hundreds of issues. The number of coloured illustrations increased over the years and lists of available titles at the back of each issue gave specific information on how many pages were printed in colour.

Predictably, colour and pigment use featured in many issues. Although not considered to be of academic value, these teach-yourself guides to colour are interesting, since Foster created a number of colour charts, wheels and palettes based on the same principles that we have seen in earlier, more serious publications on colour. Foster largely depicted his colour orders by photographing blots of oil or acrylic paints arranged on paper or canvas. Sometimes he illustrated colour mixing by depicting the act of painting in photographs or in watercolour, with hands, paintbrushes and palettes visible.

THIS IS COLOR SURPRISE GOING AROUND THE WHEEL

①

IF YOU WERE TO SQUEEZE SOME COLOR FROM A TUBE AND DIVIDE IT INTO TWO PARTS, ADDING WHITE TO ONE PART AND BLACK TO THE OTHER: AND IF THE LIGHTER ONE WAS LAID AGAINST THE DARKER ONE, IT WOULD CREATE THE ILLUSION OF LIGHT AND SHADOW OF A COLOR. THIS IS THE ESSENCE OF COLOR SURPRISE.

②

IF YOU WERE TO REPEAT THIS PROCESS, BUT AS YOU ADD WHITE ADD A BIT OF COLOR ABOVE ON THE COLOR WHEEL, YOU WOULD HAVE A RELATED SEQUENCE OF COLOR COMING TO LIGHT.

DIAL·A·COLOR
100 COLOR COMBINATIONS AT YOUR FINGERTIP

DIAL-A-COLOR is an all-purpose guide for Artists, Florists, Color Photographers, Decorators, Designers, Teachers and Others. Favorite of Everyone.

DIAL-A-COLOR is to an artisan what a compass is to the captain of a ship... a musical score to an orchestra leader... a slide rule to an engineer.

MONOCHROMATIC
A harmony made up of a single color combined with its tints, tones and shades.

ANALAGOUS
Adjacent colors that fall within a 90-degree angle on the dial.

TRIADIC
A harmony that combines three colors equi-distant on the dial.

HOW TO USE DIAL-A-COLOR
Rotate the dial below until the color you wish to use is at No. 1. Dial-A-Color explains how this color may be used effectively by itself... or as the basis of a two-color, three-color, or four-color combination.

COMPLEMENTARY
Two colors that are opposite each other on the color dial.

SPLIT-COMPLEMENTARY
One color combined with the two colors adjacent to its complement.

DOUBLE SPLIT COMPLEMENTARY
Two pairs of colors adjacent to one pair of complementary colors.

Colors on dial: 1 GREEN, 2 BLUE-GREEN, 3 BLUE, 4 BLUE-VIOLET, 5 VIOLET, 6 RED-VIOLET, 7 RED, 8 RED-ORANGE, 9 ORANGE, 10 YELLOW-ORANGE, 11 YELLOW, 12 YELLOW-GREEN

Copyright © Box 3193 Amarillo, Texas 79106

SEE OTHER SIDE

Left & above: The idea is, you turn the colour dial until your chosen colour is at the '1' position, and the information at the top of the sheet shows you various combinations, such as 'analogous' (1, 2 and 3) and 'split complementary' (1, 6 and 8). The back of the sheet offers more information about different qualities of colour.

Foster's publications undoubtedly inspired and instructed many thousands of readers. His colour wheels, charts and pigment lists are of no less historical value than those seen in more 'serious' publications, and reflect the print culture and taste of his time. The combination of minimal text and actual paints and materials captured photographically allowed Foster to explain complex concepts in a highly accessible way. On the plate 'This is Color Surprise/Going Around the Wheel', for example (see page 207), he explained the dimension of colour value in a few sentences:

If you were to squeeze some color from a tube and divide it into two parts, adding white to one part and black to the other: and if the lighter one was laid against the darker one, it would create the illusion of light and shadow of a color. This is the essence of color surprise.

After Foster's death at the age of 90, his children took over his company and continued publishing.

The company is now owned by Quarto Publishing, but Walter Foster's name is still used as a trademark for accessible instructive art manuals.

Foster's work is a prominent example of colour theory being popularised through new means of publishing, and there are many examples of colour guides and printed ephemera being produced in the later twentieth century, as colour printing became easier and cheaper. This American cardboard 'Dial-A-Color' sheet (opposite and above) from the 1960s was intended to be 'an all-purpose guide for artists, florists, color photographers, decorators, designers, teachers and others. Favorite of everyone.' On its two sides, the guide manages both to provide a spinning colour wheel and introduce several fundamental principles of colour theory, such as the trichromatic system, colour harmony, value, colour temperature, and so on. This chart is colour theory made easy, and was designed to be put up on the wall as a tool and constant source of reference.

COLOUR INTO THE FUTURE – THE WHEELS KEEP ON SPINNING

Parsons' *Tint Book* Revisited

Above: Parsons' *Tint Book* was a clever and beautifully produced reference work, offering the reader a wealth of colour schemes grouped by theme or historical period.

In 1802 Thomas Parsons founded a firm of paint and varnish makers, with premises in Long Acre in central London. The House of Parsons soon gained a reputation for supplying high-quality paint and other decorating materials. In the early twentieth century they produced small fold-out cards with samples of their ranges, including enamel paint, stressing the already long history of the firm.

In 1934 the firm, by now called Thomas Parsons & Sons Ltd and located in London's Oxford Street, published *A Tint Book of Historical Colours Suitable for Decorative Work*, containing 136 pasted-in colour samples. The firm was regularly receiving requests for reproductions of colours of the past, and the *Tint Book* was intended to address that need. Parsons pointed out the great care that had gone into producing the book, which he hoped would be 'of service to the architect, the decorative artist and the student of colour'. The book was elegantly bound with shimmering green and gold water-patterned covers and endpapers. It was essentially a very elaborate piece of advertising for the firm, since all of the paints featured in the book could be purchased from them.

The colours were grouped into 'families' of historical periods, pigment types, styles or themes, such as Colours of Egypt, Oriental Colours, Tyrian Purple, Etruscan Red and Porphyry, Pompeian Colours, Medici Blue, Moorish Colours, William & Mary, Georgian Greens, Delft Ware Colours, and so on. A colour index preceded these groups of swatches and the final chapters provided information about the firm's 'colour scheme service' and listed types of paints and enamels they could supply. Each chapter contained a short text with information about the colour group.

Parsons had to move premises during the Second World War, but continued to publish their popular *Tint Book* during the war and post-war years. It was reprinted at least six times until 1961 and is a wonderful document of a desire for rich and quality colours in interior decoration at a time when paints were often in short supply. The firm folded in the 1960s, but their book remains influential. Shortly before she died, the last director of Parsons handed the range over to the London-based paint makers Papers and Paints, founded by Robert Baty in 1960. In the 1980s his son Patrick Baty, an architectural paint historian, joined the firm and since then the Parsons colours have been reproduced as their 'Historical Colours' collection. Papers and Paints produce painted colour cards of 112 of the colours based on Parsons' tints as seen in the fourth edition from 1950. The copy shown here (above) is that fourth edition.

COLOUR INTO THE FUTURE – THE WHEELS KEEP ON SPINNING

Above right: Two small sample 'tint cards' by Thomas Parsons from the early twentieth century, when the company was still in its original premises at 8 Endell Street, Long Acre, London.

Right: Two contemporary hand-painted colour cards from Papers and Paints, London, based on Parsons' *Tint Books*.

COLOUR INTO THE FUTURE – THE WHEELS KEEP ON SPINNING

Stained Glass: New Church Architecture

Above: Sam Allen's colour key for all 460 panes of coloured glass in Basil Spence's Meeting House chapel.

Opposite: Sam Allen interprets the colour layout of Spence's fenestration in relation to the circular ground plan of the building, the movement of natural light during the day, and other ornamental and structural features.

Overleaf: The sun shines through the coloured windows of the Meeting House.

The chapel of the circular Meeting House on the Sussex University campus in the UK, built in 1966, is a striking example of how colour patterns have been used by a number of artists and architects in twentieth-century ecclesiastical architecture. Referencing the tradition of the use of stained glass in churches, the architect Sir Basil Spence employed here a language of colour, clarity and contrast, combining the shape of the circle with the colour spectrum. It owes much to the high-profile project he had finished just a few years earlier, the rebuilding of Coventry Cathedral. At Coventry Cathedral he commissioned glass features from other artists, most importantly John Hutton and John Piper, who designed the clear, engraved west window and the large, colourful Baptistry window, respectively. In keeping with the scale of the cathedral, Piper's window design was monumental and abstract, featuring a circular spectral order with a yellow centre.

In the much smaller Meeting House chapel, Spence set 460 panes of coloured glass into a honeycomb pattern of fourteen tiers of reinforced concrete blocks, illuminating the space with light that would be changing constantly according to the time of day and the seasons. When it is lit at night, the drum-shaped building resembles a lantern of coloured light from the outside.

Spence deliberately paired different materials, most prominently a surprisingly thin and therefore fragile coloured glass, which is set directly into the recesses of the roughly textured concrete blocks. He had envisaged 'a full spectrum of coloured glass panes, each in a single colour' for the chapel fenestration. However, not all windows are of a single colour. The layout roughly follows a chromatic scheme with green shades in the east, through yellow and white in the north above the altar and in alignment with the Meridian, to deep reds and blues in the west. The symbolic use of the circle is evident here, with allusions to the circle of life, the Christian year, or the unbroken circle as a manifestation of safety and security, expressed in architectural language.

The symbolism of the fenestration is subtle and open to interpretation: no area of coloured glass is separate, all shades merge into each other, and each area contains elements of the others. Crucially, no one pane is identical to another, each one a new aperture through which some of Spence's other buildings can be glimpsed. A Christian interpretation of the colour scheme is, of course, possible. For example, the yellow and white above the altar may represent divine light, while the deep red tones in the west could symbolise sacrifice and the blood of Christ. Spence did not make specific comments on colour symbolism, but he alluded to the design expressing the 'variety of the human race

COLOUR INTO THE FUTURE – THE WHEELS KEEP ON SPINNING

Blue as a spiritual colour dominates, enhanced by subtle inclusions of other primary colours

Opposite, top: Egon Eiermann's Kaiser Wilhelm Memorial Church in Berlin references long-held spiritual associations of the colour blue.

Opposite, bottom: Gerhard Richter is known for his computer-generated works of art. Here, he uses the technology to put a modern spin on traditional stained glass windows.

banded together in a circle of unity'. A couple of drawings indicate that he thought carefully about the location of each pane, laying out a key for the fenestration and even providing notes on some of the pigments used: French selenium red, orange and yellow. Spence's original chart drawings are not coloured, but in 2014 Sussex student Sam Allen made a complete colour chart of the chapel (see page 213) adding to the understanding of the deliberate colour arrangement in the space.

There are many more examples of the use of colour symbolism and colour order in the fenestration of recent church architecture, for example the hexagonal main church building and belfry of the Kaiser Wilhelm Memorial Church in Berlin (opposite, top), built between 1959 and 1963 to designs by Egon Eiermann. Like at Coventry Cathedral, the architect was briefed to create something new out of and within the ruins of the original church, which was bombed in the Second World War. Like Spence, Eiermann opted for a simple and clear combination of geometry and colour, following a specific pattern. In his design, blue as a spiritual colour dominates, enhanced by subtle inclusions of other primary colours in the individual blue squares.

An often-noted example of the use of recent coloured glass design in churches is Gerhard Richter's window for the south transept of the gothic Cologne Cathedral (opposite, bottom). The original 20-metre-tall medieval window was destroyed by bombs in the Second World War and replaced with clear glass, until Richter was commissioned to fill in the frame. In 2007 his design was revealed: a grid comprising 11,263 squares of different coloured glass, each measuring 9.6 x 9.6 cm, created from a range of 72 colours. The resulting pattern is entirely abstract and reminiscent of computer pixels. Quite deliberately so: Richter had long had an interest in colour order and specifically computer-generated colour charts, and with the Cologne Cathedral window he expressed the beauty of randomly created colour combinations. In great contrast to Spence, Piper or Eiermann – or indeed most medieval designers of church windows – his colour pattern was created randomly. Richter used a computer program to generate the colours; and the only deliberate aspect was his initial choice of colours. The visual effect of coloured light illuminating the interior remains impressive, but there is no colour symbolism to be found in Richter's window.

COLOUR INTO THE FUTURE – THE WHEELS KEEP ON SPINNING

Sky and Sea: Colour Wheels for the Natural World

In the eighteenth century, naturalists and explorers used a tool called a cyanometer to measure and record the colour of the sky. This simple handheld device, invented by Swiss physicist Horace-Bénédict de Saussure in 1789, included a numbered sequence of 53 shades of blue ranging from white to almost-black (below). The blue pigment used in the cyanometer was Prussian blue, which was invented around the turn of the eighteenth century and is considered to be the first 'modern', chemically produced and manufactured pigment.

De Saussure used the cyanometer to measure the exact blueness of the sky on hiking trips in the Alps, and the German naturalist Alexander von Humboldt, a friend of de Saussure's, took one on his voyages to South America between 1799–1804. As whimsical as the tool appears, the results of the measurements taken with it led to the scientific discovery that the colour of the sky was influenced by suspended particles in the atmosphere.

In recent times, natural colour wheels have made a comeback, this time in the art world. Spencer Finch is an American artist whose work focusses on observations of natural phenomena. Much like an early nineteenth-century landscape artist or an Impressionist painter, he meticulously records the appearance of places in changing atmospheric condition, or charts the colours he dreams of, before he transforms these observations and memories into a new medium, for example photography, drawings and moving images. Often the results are abstract paintings in oil or watercolour, and sometimes more complex installations incorporating lightboxes and filters. In one work he recorded colours he had perceived in his dreams and then produced blot paintings in matching colours, thereby creating a link between an entirely subjective perception and a material expression of it.

In 2010 Finch observed the colour of the sea on the south coast of England for several weeks and assigned a Pantone® colour to each hue he noted. When he had observed 100 different shades he dyed 100 flags in these monochrome colours. He also created a spinning colour wheel with these 100 Pantone swatches along its edge and a static aperture (opposite). The installation, titled *The Colour of Water*, was erected at Folkestone, Kent, looking out over the English Channel, on the occasion of the town's second art Triennial, in 2011. Each morning of the Triennial, an observer identified the colour of the sea and the flag of the corresponding colour was flown in the town. The flags are no longer there, but the colour wheel remains, inviting passers-by to observe and record the colour of the sea at the time of their visit.

This pair of wheels is a good example of the subtle overlap between art and science across several centuries. Both are relatively simple, man-made tools that help capture and chart observations of natural phenomena. Both are at once exciting in the range of tints displayed on them, but at the same time a glance at them also induces a sense of the impossibility of capturing all the nuances of the natural world. The sea clearly appears in more colours than the 100 contained in the wheel, and there are certainly more than 53 shades of sky blue. The wheels are also beautiful objects in their own right, an expression of humankind's desire to understand, find patterns and see order, but both are ultimately crude and conceptual rather than exact. Romantic artists were known to observe atmospheric conditions meticulously and accurately, often consulting scientific tools and academic literature – but expressed in painting. Finch has created a measuring tool that can be used according to this function, but it was always intended to be a work of art and ultimately refers back to the subjectivity of colour perception.

Right: The cyanometer, first used in the eighteenth century, was invented as a tool for recording the precise shade of blue seen in the sky.

Opposite: Spencer Finch's *The Colour of Water* installation featured a kind of modern-day cyanometer. This one is not systematically ordered, and it was designed for noting the colour of the sea rather than the sky.

The Rainbow Lives On: Newton's Legacy in Contemporary Art and Culture

Nowadays many people probably associate the image of a prism refracting light into rainbow colours with Pink Floyd rather than Isaac Newton

Opposite: Pink Floyd's iconic The Dark Side of the Moon packaging references Newton's groundbreaking experiment, including the prism and white light but, like so many others, omitting indigo and depicting only six spectral colours.

Isaac Newton has inspired art and artists ever since he unravelled the rainbow in the late seventeenth century. The spectral range of colours, created from light but often experienced and explained in the context of darkness, has become one of the most recognisable concepts and images of the modern world. It is a pure, simple and universal order that can be expressed in many ways but is most commonly visualised as a scale, a ring, a wheel, or as light entering and exiting a prism. As a diagram, it has strong visual and conceptual qualities that make it a popular motif in many forms, genres and subjects of art and culture, particularly in graphic design.

A literal take on Newton's experiment of splitting white light with the help of a prism was the inspiration for the now iconic vinyl record sleeve of British band Pink Floyd's 1973 album *The Dark Side of the Moon* (opposite). It was designed at the Hipgnosis studio in London by Storm Thorgerson, using commissioned artwork by illustrator George Hardie. Against a background of deep unstructured black we see the outlines of a prism, represented as an equilateral triangle, suggestive of the darkness of Newton's studio and possibly also in reference to the theme of the album title. A thin white line of light enters the triangle from the left and emerges on the other side as six spectral colours (in a deviation from Newton's proposed seven colours, omitting indigo, as do many painters' colour wheels). This band of colours bleeds onto the inside of the double sleeve, where it morphs into an image of acoustic wavelengths, thus continuing the tradition of drawing analogies between colour, music and rhythm, as Newton himself had done. In this context the imagery referred specifically to the audio, visual and sensual experience of Pink Floyd's live performances, which included elaborate light shows. The sleeve art of *The Dark Side of the Moon* became so popular that Thorgerson quipped shortly before his death in 2013 that nowadays many people probably associate the image of a prism refracting light into rainbow colours with Pink Floyd rather than Isaac Newton.

Above: Tyree Callahan's *Chromatic Typewriter* (2013) plays with the idea of being able to 'write colour'. The colour order Callahan depicts riffs on upper-case/lower-case variations in type.

Many contemporary artists directly or indirectly refer to Newton's spectrum, using the universal beauty of pure colour order and symbolic associations with rainbows. American artist Tyree Callahan has superimposed the colours of the visible spectrum onto a 1930s manual typewriter (above), thus creating the concept of an alphabet of colour and a mechanical system of producing paintings. One could criticise the very idea of mechanical production of daubs of paint, but there is a nice coincidence here in Newton having been criticised in the early nineteenth century for de-romanticising the rainbow by applying hard science to it. Callahan's *Chromatic Typewriter* is just another way of ordering colour, and is not dissimilar to the arrangement of colour in paint boxes, on palettes, or in diagrams, but here it is embedded in conceptual art.

Mexican-born artist Gabriel Dawe 'weaves' rainbows into architectural spaces, using only coloured thread, narrow panels of wood and small hooks, creating sculptural pieces that give the impression of beams of coloured light and challenge notions of materiality and immateriality (opposite). The materiality is definite and double in meaning: each piece is made from dyed thread, and each piece is contructed specially for the place it will be shown. From a distance, however, it appears as coloured light, and the colours mix in the eye, distinct only when viewed up close. This series of woven rainbows is titled *Plexus*, a medical term for the complex interlacing network of nerves or blood vessels. Although not intentionally referencing Newton or colour order, Dawe notes that '*Plexus* evokes the intrinsic order within the apparent chaos that exists in nature.'

The ephemeral and immaterial nature of coloured light, and rainbows in particular, adds another symbolic dimension to the colour spectrum. Many conceptual and installation artists have tried to create ways of making the intangible tangible. Coloured light plays a key role in the art of the Icelandic-Danish artist Olafur Eliasson, who has often experimented with

Above: Gabriel Dawe's *Plexus* at the Renwick Gallery of the Smithsonian American Art Museum in 2015. Though comprising only fifteen colours of thread, it represents the full spectrum of visible light,

chromatic order in various formations; for example in the *Colour Spectrum Series* in 2005, where he placed neat rectangles of framed colours in a linear rainbow pattern on the walls of the exhibition space, or the later glassy colour circle *Polychromatic Attention* (overleaf, page 223) in 2015. Eliasson's colour wheels in the *Turner Colour Experiments* series, painted in 2014 for Tate Britain in response to J. M. W. Turner's use of light and colour across seven paintings, bear an uncanny resemblance to Chevreul's lithographs in *Cercles Chromatique* (see pages 98–101). In a direct nod to Newton, Eliasson has also created circular rainbows in darkened rooms using lenses and projectors.

In larger-scale installation projects Eliasson has succeeded in creating spaces in which visitors can physically immerse themselves in the colour spectrum. The most ambitious of these is *Your Rainbow Panorama* (overleaf, page 224) a rainbow walkway 150 metres in length, constructed from timber, steel and coloured glass, installed on the top of the ARoS Aarhus Kunstmuseum in Denmark between 2006 and 2011. Here, museum visitors can walk in a perfect circle through the entire visible spectrum of colours, the city around them changing colour as they move. From the street below and other vantage points in the city the transparent perfect colour circle is visible, seemingly suspended, as if it is just about to land on the building, with silhouetted human figures walking through it, its colours constantly changing according to the intensity and angle of the sunlight.

COLOUR INTO THE FUTURE – THE WHEELS KEEP ON SPINNING

222 COLOUR INTO THE FUTURE – THE WHEELS KEEP ON SPINNING

Left, top & bottom: *Your Rainbow Panorama* is a walkway of coloured glass on the roof of the ARoS Aarhus Kunstmuseum in Denmark, a large-scale and immersive interpretation of the visible spectrum, which can be experienced from the inside as well as viewed from a distance.

Above: Eliasson's *Polychromatic Attention*, an installation from 2015, is a colour circle of 24 crystal-glass spheres, forming a complete ring of the visible spectrum in graded hues. The hues are created by concave sheets of coloured chrome, inserted into the spheres. The highly reflective surfaces of this work visually blur the boundaries of light, water and solid materials.

Falling Back in Love with Colour

Above & opposite: David Batchelor's *Magic Hour* (above) and *Chromocochere* (opposite) use video to bring immaterial colour and art together. In previous centuries, it would have been hard to think of colour in art as anything but material – the use of pigments on a ground such as paper or canvas.

David Batchelor is a British artist who focusses on ideas about colour in both his art and his writing. But it wasn't always the case; in fact the absence of colour has inspired him as much as colour itself. In a recent publication, *The Luminous and the Grey* (2014), he explained that for about twenty years he didn't consider colour worth thinking about, quietly accepting the preference for black and white in late twenthieth-century conceptual art. His early work included, perhaps predictably, monochromatic canvasses and timber-and-glass constructions in either black or white. He 'discovered' colour quite by chance, by impulsively adding a vibrant magenta colour to one side of a small piece of a sculpture in 1993, which then stood out sharply against the otherwise black-and-white interiors of his studio, making him question the absence of colour in contemporary art and design. He then began embracing colour artistically, conceptually and intellectually, but at the heart of his work as a writer and artist, is the exploration of our ambivalent relationship with colour.

In 2000 Batchelor published the extended essay *Chromophobia*, in which he discussed the current obsession with white spaces in the West – and the long-standing aversion to colour. Reading and rereading historic colour literature, such as Charles Blanc's *Grammaire des arts du dessin architecture, sculpture, peinture* from 1867, he found a long tradition of colour avoidance and fear of colour. *Chromophobia* is a quietly shocking and beautifully composed argument against the marginalisation of colour as feminine, dangerous, secondary, primitive or a mere ornamental addition. Batchelor has also edited an anthology of excerpts from colour literature since 1846, which gave him a particularly strong understanding of our complex relationship with colour and how ideas about colour are expressed in writing. *The Luminous and the Grey* also deals with those liminal spaces where colour begins or ceases to exist; the non-colour grey, associated with death, decay and absence.

In Batchelor's art, both two- and three-dimensional, intense pure colour, including black and white, illumination and colour order are recurring and dominant features. The influence of colour theory is particularly prominent in a 2015 installation titled *Chromocochere* (opposite), a large LED-lit colour ring of changing hues that was mounted on the entrance to the MK Gallery in Milton Keynes in the UK. The colour ring was illuminated in single intense colours, going through the complete spectrum within each full hour. Earlier work such as *Magic Hour* (above), from 2004–2007, also shows spectral colours in a fluorescent starburst pattern, emanating from found lightboxes that were stacked up, facing a white wall in a darkened room. It is tempting, and perhaps intended, to associate this installation with Newton's experiments with prisms and light in a darkened room, or to think of his rival Goethe's argument that colour is created in the space where light and darkness meet.

COLOUR INTO THE FUTURE – THE WHEELS KEEP ON SPINNING 225

Pantone® Sets a Colour Standard

Today there are many systems in place that help us choose and combine colours in art, design, printing, interior decoration and branding. Many companies that deal in colours and paints produce charts, sheets or catalogues with colour samples, from simple ranges that reflect the choice of ready-made housepaints available, to more elaborate ones that can be made to order. A few companies, such as Pantone, aim to provide comprehensive standardised colour systems that can be used internationally in design, branding, printing, industrial production and the arts. In 1963, Pantone revolutionised the printing industry with the colourful Pantone Matching System®, an innovative tool allowing for the faithful selection, articulation and reproduction of consistent, accurate colour anywhere in the world. The tool organises colour standards through a proprietary numbering system and chip format, which have since become iconic to the Pantone brand.

Since the company introduced its first colour guides, it has become an established industry authority on colour, widely used by the print industry, but it has also become a tastemaker. Conducting consumer colour preference research since 1986, the Pantone Color Institute studies the role of colour in psychology and design, making the world of colour charts, guides and lists relevant in new ways. Calling out the top ten colors at NY Fashion Week since 1993, many now use the Pantone Color Institute for their seasonal colour direction. Since 2000 the Pantone Color Insitute has been selecting a 'colour of the year', reflecting what is taking place in our global culture at a particular moment in time, bringing colour and the colour industry into the realms of the press and social media. Understanding that colour is lifestyle, Pantone also offers consumer products including a range of stationery, mugs and other products that showcase the colors contained in the different Pantone Colour Systems.

Opposite: Pantone's Formula Series fan deck, including 1,867 Pantone spot colors and providing the ink formulation for each.

COLOUR INTO THE FUTURE – THE WHEELS KEEP ON SPINNING

Glossary

Additive Colour See *Immaterial Colour*. See also *Material Colour*.

Analogous Colour
Analogous colours are groups of three colours that lie next to each other on the *Colour Wheel*. One is *Primary*, one is *Secondary* and one is *Tertiary*.

Aquatint
A printmaking technique where tonal effects are produced by using acid to 'eat into' the printing plate, creating sunken areas which hold the ink.

Bauhaus
Bauhaus was a revolutionary school of art, architecture and design established in Germany in 1919. Its aim was to bring together the fine and applied arts and its style was radically minimalist, promoting clean lines, pure colours and strong materials. Bauhaus incorporated colour theory in its teaching and practice.

CIELAB
This is a system for numerically defining and communicating all the colours visible to the human eye, published in 1976 by the International Commission on Illumination.

Chroma See also *HVC, Saturation*.
Chroma, a term first used by Munsell, denotes the *Saturation* or brilliance of a colour. Highly chromatic colours contain maximum *Hue* with few impurities or additives such as white, grey or black. A colour without hue is called 'achromatic' or 'monochromatic' and appears grey.

CMYK See also *RGB*.
A colour system that is used mostly in printed design. Modern colour theory determined that the three colours that combine most effectively are cyan, magenta and yellow (CMY). With the advent of photomechanical printing, black ink was added and the system was named CMYK (cyan, magenta, yellow and black).

Colour Wheel
A circular diagram that is used to show the relationships between Primary, Secondary, Tertiary and Complementary colours. Since Isaac Newton first popularised this visual aid to explain colour, many different versions, not all of them round, have been proposed.

Complementary Colour
Complementary colours appear opposite each other on the Colour Wheel. The colour complement of each Primary Colour can be obtained by mixing the two other primary colours together.

Enlightenment
An intellectual and philosophical movement originating in Europe in the seventeenth century and spanning the eighteenth century. Freedom, democracy and reason were advocated as the primary values of society.

Engraving
A printmaking technique that involves making incisions into a metal plate, traditionally copper, with a sharp tool. Ink is rolled onto the plate and the incisions retain the ink and form the printed image when transferred to paper.

Etching
Etching is a printmaking technique where a plate, traditionally copper, is covered with varnish, then a design is scratched through it. Acid is applied to the plate and affects only the exposed metal, etching the design onto the plate. The varnish is removed and the plate inked for transfer to paper.

Fauvism
A movement by artists including Henri Matisse and André Derain from around 1905 to 1910, characterised by strong colours and loose brushwork.

Hue
The attribute commonly described as colour; that which makes it discernible as red or green, and so on. Hues are dependent on the dominant wavelength of light that is emitted or reflected from an object and are independent of *Saturation* or *Tone*. Pure white, black and greys have no hue.

HVC (Hue, Value, Chroma)
A numerical colour system expressed using a flexible three-dimensional model that was devised by Munsell and based on three identifiable and measurable qualities of colour: *Hue*, *Chroma* and Value (*Tone*).

Immaterial Colour Also known as *Additive Colour*. See also *Material Colour*.
Immaterial, or Additive, colour is created by mixing different colours of light. Red, green and blue are the most commonly used immaterial primary colours, and if the same intensity of all these are overlapped, white light results. Immaterial colours are the basis of all colours used on screen.

Impressionism
Impressionism is an art movement developed in France in the nineteenth century and is based on the practice of painting rapidly outside (*en plein air*) rather than in a studio from sketches. This spontaneous method resulted in a greater awareness of light and colour.

Industrial Revolution
The Industrial Revolution was the transition to new manufacturing processes. In this time, from about 1760 to sometime between 1820 and 1840, rural societies in Europe and America became industrial and urban.

Intensity See *Saturation*.

Lithography
Lithography is printing process based on the antipathy of grease and water. A flat stone or metal plate is treated with a greasy medium so as to repel ink except where it is required for printing.

Material Colour Also known as *Subtractive Colour*. See also *Immaterial Colour*.
Material or Subtractive colours are used in painting and are associated with the reflection and absorption of light. The material *Primary Colours* are red,

blue and yellow and different colours result when these colours are combined, each due to some wavelengths of light being partially or completely subtracted (that is, absorbed). Exactly equal amounts of red, blue and yellow produce black.

Monochromatic
The term 'monochromatic' means containing or using only one colour with varying *Tones* or shades of it, although it is often used loosely to describe works in which a single colour predominates. It is also used to mean a colour without *Hue*, which appears grey.

Optical Mixing
Optical mixing is when two different colours placed side by side appear to create a different colour. The Impressionists (and other groups) used this technique rather than pre-mixing paint colours on a palette.

Orphism
Orphism was an abstract offshoot of Cubism developed by Robert and Sonia Delaunay around 1912, which gave priority to light and colour.

Picturesque See also *Romantic* and *Sublime*.
The term 'picturesque', often applied to landscapes in the eighteenth century, referred to an ideal that is beautiful but has some elements of wildness. Earlier in the eighteenth century, aesthetic ideas favoured either the *Sublime* at one extreme (awesome sights such as great mountains) or, at the other extreme, beautiful, peaceful, even pretty sights. Picturesque came in between.

Pigment
The pigment is the element in paint that provides its colour. Pigments can be made from a wide range of materials including minerals, natural and synthetic dyes, and other man-made compounds.

Primary Colours Also known as *Primitive Colours, Pure Colours*.
The primary colours vary depending on the type of colour system. The painting colour system which is Material or subtractive includes red, yellow and blue (RYB), the three pigment colours that cannot be formed by any combination of other colours. Red, green and blue (RGB) colours are the primaries of the Immaterial or additive system.

Primitive Colours See *Primary Colours*.

Pure Colours See *Primary Colours*.

RGB See also *CMYK*.
This is an Immaterial or additive colour system in which red, green and blue light is added together to produce a full range of colours. This system is the basis of all colours used on screen.

Romantic See also *Picturesque* and *Sublime*.
The term 'Romantic' when used to describe a period or style applies to art, literature and music chiefly of the late eighteenth and early nineteenth century, exhibiting certain characteristics such as individuality, emotion, drama and an interest in the natural world. Romanticism represented a shift away from the restraint of Classicism.

Saturation Also known as *Intensity*.
Also known as intensity, saturation describes the strength of a colour with respect to its Tone or lightness and describes how bold or pale a colour looks under different light conditions. Commonly used as a synonym for *Chroma* especially in graphic arts.

Secondary Colours Also known as *Compound Colours*.
The colours produced by combining or mixing two *Primary Colours*. Since the *Immaterial* and *Material Colour* systems have different primary colours, their secondary colours vary too.

Spectral Colours
These are the colours visible to the human eye when white light is split, as in Newton's experiments splitting white light using a prism. Individual colours are evoked by a single wavelength of light in the Visible Spectrum. Spectral colours, as in a rainbow, are most commonly arranged from violet with the shortest wavelength to red with the longest. Related to *Immaterial Colour*.

Sublime See also *Picturesque* and *Romantic*.
The sublime is an impression of grandeur, awe and fear, and theories about conveying it were developed by Edmund Burke and other thinkers in the mid-eighteenth century. Burke defined the sublime as an artistic effect that produces the strongest emotion the mind is capable of feeling. To evoke the sublime, he advocated darkness and gloom in painting and architecture and advised against gaudiness induced by the use of colour.

Subtractive Colour See *Material Colour*. See also *Immaterial Colour*.

Tertiary Colours
The colours produced by combining or mixing a *Primary* and a *Secondary Colour* such as red and green or two secondary colours such as green and orange. Combining two secondaries results in muddy colours: browns, greys and blacks. On the *Colour Wheel* it may also refer to a subtler gradation between primaries and secondaries such as olive green.

Tone Also known as *Value*.
Tone refers to the relative lightness or darkness of a colour, its brightness, rather than the colour or *Hue* itself.

Value See *Tone*.

Visible Spectrum
The visible spectrum is the portion of the electromagnetic spectrum that is visible to the human eye. See also *Spectral Colour*.

Bibliography

Ackermann, Rudolph, *The Repository of Arts, Literature, Commerce, Manufactures, Fashions and Politics* (Published monthly, London: 1809–1828).

Albers, Josef, *Interaction of Color* (New Haven: Yale University Press, 1963; paperback edition, 1971).
———*Interaction of Color: New Complete Edition* (New Haven: Yale University Press, 2009).

Arrowsmith, Henry William and A., *The House Decorator and Painter's Guide; Containing a Series of Designs for Decorating Apartments, Suited to the Various Styles of Architecture* (London: Thomas Kelly, 1850).

Baretti, Joseph, *A Guide Through the Royal Academy, By Joseph Baretti Secretary For Foreign Correspondence To The Royal Academy* (London: printed by T. Cadwell c. 1781).

Barnard, George, *The Theory and Practice of Landscape Painting in Water-Colours* (London: Hamilton, Adams & Co., 1855; 2nd edition, 1858).

Batchelor, David, *Chromophobia* (London: Reaktion Books Ltd, 2000).
———(ed.) *Colour: Documents of Contemporary Art* (London: Whitechapel Gallery and Cambridge, Mass: The MIT Press, 2018).
——— *The Luminous and the Grey* (London: Reaktion Books Ltd, 2014).

Benson, William, *Principles of the Science of Colour, Concisely Stated to Aid and Promote their Useful Application in the Decorative Arts* (London: Chapman and Hall, 1868).

Birren, Faber, *The Color Primer: A Basic Treatise on the Color System of Wilhelm Ostwald/A Grammar of Color: A Basic Treatise on the Color System of Albert H. Munsell/Principles of Color: A Review of Past Traditions and Modern Theories of Color Harmony* (New York: Van Nostrand Reinhold, 1969).

Blanc, Charles, *Grammaire des arts du dessin architecture, sculpture, peinture* (Paris: Jules Renouard, 1867).

Boutet, Claude (attr.), *Traité de la peinture en mignature pour apprendre aisément à peindre sans maître* (The Hague: van Dole, 1708).

British Colour Council, *The British Colour Council Dictionary of Colour Standards: A List of Colour Names Referring to the Colours Shown in the Companion Volume* (London: British Colour Council, 1934).

Burke, Edmund, *A Philosophical Enquiry into the Origin of Our Ideas of the Sublime and Beautiful* (London: printed for R. and J. Dodsley, in Pall-Mall, 1757).

Burnet, John, *Practical Hints on Colour in Painting* (London: J. Carpenter & Son, 1827).

Campbell, Richard, *The London Tradesman* (London: printed by T. Gardner, 1747).

Carpenter, Henry Barrett, *Suggestions for the Study of Colour* (Rochdale: H. B. Carpenter, 1923).

Cawse, John, *The Art of Painting Portraits, Landscapes, Animals, Draperies, Satins, &c. in Oil Colours: Practically Explained by Coloured Palettes* (London: Rudolph Ackermann, 1840).
———*Introduction to the Art of Painting in Oil Colours* (London: printed for R. Ackermann, 1822).

Cennini, Cennino (author), Mary Philadelphia Merrifield (translator), Signor Tambroni (introduction and notes), *A Treatise on Painting, Written by Cennino Cennini in the Year 1437* (London: E. Lumley, 1844; first published in Italian in 1821).

Chevreul, Michel Eugène, *Atlas. Expose d'un moyen de definir et de nommer les couleurs d'après une méthode précise et expérimentale: avec l'application de ce moyen a la définition et a la dénomination des couleurs d'un grand nombre de corps naturels et de produits artificiels* (Paris: Didot, 1861).
———*Des couleurs et de leurs applications aux arts industriels à l'aide des cercles chromatiques* (Paris: J. B. Baillière & fils, 1864)
——— *De la loi du contraste simultané des couleurs et de l'assortiment des objets colorés: considéré d'après cette loi dans ses rapports avec la peinture, les tapisseries des gobelins, les tapisseries de Beauvais pour meubles, les tapis, la mosaique, les vitraux colorés, l'impression des étoffes, l'imprimerie, l'enluminure, la décoration des édifices, l'habillement et l'horticulture* (Paris: Pitois-Levrault et cie, 1839).
———*The Principles of Harmony and Contrast of Colours, and Their Applications to the Arts: Including Painting, Interior Decoration, Tapestries, Carpets, Mosaics, Coloured Glazing, Paper-staining, Calico-printing, Letterpress Printing, Map-colouring, Dress, Landscape and Flower Gardening, Etc. Tr. from the French by Charles Martel* (London: Longman, Brown, Green and Lo§ngmans, 1854).

Chevreul, Michel Eugène and René Henri Digeon, *Cercles chromatiques de M.E. Chevreul* (Paris: E. Thunot, 1855).

Cox, David, *A Series of Progressive Lessons, Intended to Elucidate the Art of Landscape Painting in Water Colours* (London: T. Clay, No. 18, Ludgate Hill, London, printed by J. Hayes, 1811).
———*The Young Artist's Companion or, Drawing-book of Studies and Landscape Embellishments: Comprising a Great Variety of the Most Picturesque Objects Required in Various Compositions of Landscape Scenery Arranged as Progressive Lessons* (London: S. & J. Fuller, 1825).

Curwen, Harold, *Printing* [Puffin Picture Book series] (London: Penguin, 1948).

de Lemos, Pedro Joseph, *Applied Art: Drawing, Painting, Design and Handicraft* (California: Pacific Press Publishing Association, 1920; reissued 1933).

Doerner, Max, *The Materials of the Artist and their Use in Painting, with Notes on the Techniques of the Old Masters* (New York: Harcourt Brace and Company, 1934).
——— *Malmaterial und seine Verwendung in Bilde: nach den Vorträgen an der Akademie der bildenden Künste in München* (München: Verlag für praktische Kunstwissenschaft, 1921).

Field, George, *Chromatics, or, An Essay on the Analogy and Harmony of Colours* (London: printed for the author by A. J. Valpy, Tooke's Court, Chancery Lane; and sold by Mr. Newman, Soho Square, 1817).
——— *Chromatographie. Eine Abhandlung über Farben und Pigmente, so wie deren Anwendung in der Malerkunst etc.* (Weimar: Verlage des Landes-Industrie-Comptoirs, 1836).
——— *Chromatography, or, A Treatise on Colours and Pigments, and of their Powers in Painting, &c.* (London: Tilt and Bogue, Fleet Street, 1835).
——— *Rudiments of the Painters' Art: or A Grammar of Colouring, Applicable to Operative Painting, Decorative Architecture, and the Arts*, 2nd edition (London: John Weale, 1858).

Fielding, Theodore Henry, *Index of Colours and Mixed Tints for the use of Beginners in Landscape and Figure Painting* (London: printed for the author, 1830).
——— *On Painting in Oil and Water Colours for Landscape and Portraits* (London: Ackermann and Co., 1839).

Fischer, Martin, *The Permanent Palette* (Maryland and New York: National Publishing Society, 1930).

Gartside, Mary, *An Essay on a New Theory of Colours, and on Composition in General, Illustrated by Coloured Blots Shewing the Application of the Theory to Composition of Flowers, Landscapes, Figures, &c.* (London: T. Gardiner, W. Miller and I. and A. Arch, 1808).
——— *An Essay on Light and Shade, on Colours, and on Composition in General* (London, printed for the author, by T. Davison, and sold by T. Gardiner, 1805).

Gilpin, William, *Hints to Form the Taste & Regulate ye Judgment in Sketching Landscape*, ca. *1790*. Manuscript, Yale Center for British Art, Paul Mellon Collection, ND1340 G5, 1790.
———*Three Essays: On Picturesque Beauty, on Picturesque Travel and on Sketching Landscape. To Which is Added a Poem, on Landscape Painting* (London: Printed for R. Blamire, in the Strand, 1792).

Goethe, Johann Wolfgang von, *Beyträge zur Optik* (Weimar: Im Verlage des Industrie Comptoirs, 1791/1972).
———*Theory of Colours*; translated with notes by Charles Lock Eastlake (London: J. Murray, 1840).
———*Zur Farbenlehre* [3 vols] (Tübingen: J. G. Cotta'sche Buchhandlung, 1810–1812).

Griffits, Thomas E., *The Technique of Colour Printing by Lithography: A Concise Manual of Drawn Lithography* (London: Faber & Faber Ltd, 1948).

Harris, Moses, *An Exposition of English Insects: Including the Several Classes of Neuroptera, & Hymenoptera, & Diptera, or Bees, Flies, & Libellula* (London: printed for the author, sold by Mr. White, bookseller, in Fleet-Street, and Mr. Robson, in New Bond Street, 1776 [1782]).
———*The Natural System of Colours, Wherein is Displayed the Regular and Beautiful Order and Arrangement, Arising from the Three Primitives [sic], Red, Blue, and Yellow* (London: Laidler, c. 1769–1776).
———*The Natural System of Colours, Wherein is Displayed the Regular and Beautiful Order and Arrangement, Arising from the Three Primitives, Red, Blue, and Yellow*. New edition with additions by Thomas Martyn (London: Harrison and Leigh, 1811).

Hay, David Ramsay, *The Laws of Harmonious Colouring, Adapted to Interior Decorations, Manufactures, and Other Useful Purposes*, 5th edition (London; W. S. Orr and Co, 1844).
———*A Nomenclature of Colours, Hues, Tints, and Shades, Applicable to the Arts and Natural Sciences; to Manufactures, and other Purposes of General Utility* (William Blackwood and Sons, 1845).

Hayter, Charles, *A New Practical Treatise on the Three Primitive Colours* (London: J. Innes, 1826).

Hogarth, William, *The Analysis of Beauty, Written with a View of Fixing the Fluctuating Ideas of Taste* (London: printed by J. Reeves for the Author, 1753).

Hope, Thomas, *Household Furniture and Interior Decoration, Executed from Designs* (London: Longman, Hurst, Rees, & Orme, 1807).

Howard, Frank, *Colour as a Means of Art: Being an Adaptation of the Experience of Professors to the Practice of Amateurs* (London: Joseph Thomas, 1838).
———*The Sketcher's Manual; or, The Whole Art of Picture Making Reduced to the Simplest Pinciples* (London: Darton and Clark, 1837).

Ibbetson, Julius, *An Accidence, or Gamut, of Painting in Oil and Water Colours* (London: for the author by Darton and Harvey, 1803).

Itten, Johannes, *The Art of Color: The Subjective Experience and Objective Rationale of Color*; translated by Ernst van Haagen, 2nd edition (New York: Van Nostrand Reinhold, 1962).
———*Kunst der Farbe: Subjektives Erleben und objektives Erkennen als Wege zur Kunst* (Ravensburg: Otto Maier, 1961).

Jacobs, Michel, *The Art of Colour* (London: William Heinemann, 1925; first published in 1923, New York: Garden City).

[continued overleaf]

Jones, Owen, *The Grammar of Ornament* (London: Day & Son, 1856).

Kandinsky, Wassily, *Über das Geistige in der Kunst, insbesondere in der Malerei*, 2nd edition (München: R. Piper, 1912).

Klee, Paul, *Pädagogisches Skizzenbuch* (München: Albert Langen, 1925).
———*Beiträge zur bildnerischen Formlehre*, edited by Jürgen Glaesemer (Basel/Stuttgart: Paul Klee-Stiftung, 1979).

Lacouture, Charles, *Répertoire chromatique: solution raisonnée et pratique des problèmes les plus usuels dans l'étude et l'emploi des couleurs* (Paris: Gauthier-Villars, 1890).

Lambert, Johann Heinrich, *Beschreibung einer mit dem Calauschen Wachse ausgemalten Farbenpyramide, wo die Mischung jeder Farben aus Weiß und drei Grundfarben angeordnet* (Berlin: Haude und Spener, 1772).

Le Blon, Jacob Christoph, *Coloritto, or, The Harmony of Colouring in Painting / L'Harmonie du coloris dans la peinture* […] (London: [publisher not identified], 1725).

[Le Blon, Jacob Christoph] Gautier de Montdorge, Antoine, *L'art d'imprimer les tableaux : traité d'après les écrits, les opérations & les instructions verbales de J. C. Le Blon.* (Paris: Ches P.G. Le Mercier [etc.], 1756).

Leonardo da Vinci, *A Treatise on Painting* (London: Senex and Taylor, 1721).

Mérimée, Jean-François-Léonor, *The Art of Painting in Oil and in Fresco: Being a History of the Various Processes and Materials Employed from its Discovery, by Hubert and John Van Eyck, to the Present Time/Translated from the Original French Treatise of J.F.L. Mérimée, with original observations on the rise and progress of British art, the French and English chromatic scales, and theories of colouring, by W.B. Sarsfield Taylor* (London: Whittaker, 1839).

———*De la peinture à l'huile, ou Des procédés matériels employés dans ce genre de peinture, depuis Hubert et Jean Van-Eyck jusqu'à nos jours* (Paris: Mme Huzard, 1830).

Merrifield, Mary Philadelphia, 'The Harmony of Colors as Exemplified in the Exhibition', in: *The Art Journal Illustrated Catalogue: The Industry of All Nations* (London: published for the proprietors by George Virtue, 1851).

Munsell, A. H., *Atlas of the Munsell Color System* (Malden, MA: printed by Wadsworth, Howland & Co., c. 1915).
———*A Color Notation. A measured color system, based on the three qualities Hue, Value and Chroma* (Boston: Geo. H. Ellis Co., 1905; 5th edition, New York: Munsell Color Company, 1919).
———*A Grammar of Color: Arrangements of Strathmore Papers in a Variety of Printed Color Combinations According to the Munsell Color System* (Mittineague, Mass.: The Strathmore Paper Company, 1921).

Newton, Sir Isaac, *Opticks: or, A Treatise of the Reflexions, Refractions, Inflexions and Colours of Light* (London: Sam. Smith & Benj. Walford, 1704).

Oram, William, *Precepts and Observations on the Art of Colouring in Landscape Painting* (London: printed for White and Cochranne by Richard Taylor, 1810).

Ostwald, Wilhelm, *Die Farbenfibel* (Leipzig: Unesma, 1917).
———*Die Harmonie der Farben* (Leipzig: Verlag Unesma, 1918).
———*Letters to a Painter on the Theory and Practice of Painting*; translated by H. W. Morse. (Boston/New York/Chicago/London: Ginn & Company. 1907).
———*Malerbriefe. Beiträge Zur Theorie und Praxis der Malerei* (Leipzig: Verlag von S. Hirzel, 1904).

Parsons, Thomas, *A Tint Book of Historical Colours*, 4th edition (London: Thomas Parsons & Sons, 1934; 1950).

Piot, René, *Les palettes de Delacroix* (Paris: 1930).

Repton, Humphry, *Fragments on the Theory and Practice of Landscape Gardening* (London: printed by T. Bensley and Son, Bolt Court, Fleet Street; for J. Taylor, at the Architectural Library, High Holborn, 1816).
———*Observations on the Theory and Practice of Landscape Gardening* (London: printed by T. Bensley and Son, Bolt Court, Fleet Street; for J. Taylor, at the Architectural Library, High Holborn, 1803).

Rood, Ogden Nicholas, *Colour: A Text-Book of Modern Chromatics with Applications to Art and Industry*, 3rd edition (London: Kegan Paul, Trench, Trubner, [1st ed. as below]; 1890).
———*Modern Chromatics, with Applications to Art and Industry* (New York: D. Appleton and Company, 1879).

Runge, Philipp Otto, *Die Farben-Kugel, oder Konstruktion des Verhältnisses aller Mischungen der Farben zu einander, und ihrer vollständigen Affinität, mit angehängtem Versuch einer Ableitung der Harmonie in den Zusammenstellungen der Farben* (Hamburg: Friedrich Perthes, 1810).

Schiffermüller, Ignaz, *Versuch eines Farbensystems* (Vienna: Agustin Bernardi, 1772).

Schopenhauer, Arthur, *Über das Sehn und die Farbe* (Leipzig: Johann Friedrich Hartnoch, 1816).
———*Über das Sehn und die Farbe*, revised and extended edition (Leipzig: Johann Friedrich Hartnoch, 1854).

Scott Taylor, J., *The Simple Explanation of the Ostwald Colour System* (London: Winsor & Newton, 1935).

Senefelder, Alois, *A Complete Course of Lithography* (London: Ackermann, 1819).

Sol, J. C. M., *La palette theorique: ou, Classification des couleurs* (Vannes: N. de Lamarzelle, 1849).

Sowerby, James, *A New Elucidation of Colours, Original, Prismatic and Material; Showing their Concordance in Three Primitives, Yellow, Red, and Blue; and the Means of Producing Measuring and Mixing Them: with Some Observations on the Accuracy of Sir Isaac Newton* (London: Richard Taylor & Co. 1809).

Syme, Patrick (editor), *Werner's Nomenclature of Colours, With Additions, Arranged so as to Render it Highly Useful to the Arts and Sciences, Particularly Zoology, Botany, Chemistry, Mineralogy, and Morbid Anatomy. Annexed to Which Are Examples Selected From Well-known Objects in the Animal, Vegetable, and Mineral Kingdoms* (Edinburgh: William Blackwood, and London: John Murray and Robert Baldwin, 1814; London: T. Cadell, 1821).

Turner, Joseph Mallord William, 'Color', from *Royal Academy Lectures by Joseph Mallord William Turner, R.A., as Professor of Perspective and Geometry, a Post to Which he Was Elected 10 Dec. 1807 and Which He Resigned 10 Feb. 1838.* Manuscript, British Library Add MS 46151 A-BB: 1806–1902; transcribed and printed in J. Gage, *Colour in Turner: Poetry and Truth* (London: Studio Vista, 1969), pp. 196–197.

Wittgenstein, Ludwig, *Bemerkungen über die Farben / Remarks on Colour*; edited by G. E. M. Anscombe, translated by Linda L. McAlister and Margaret Schattle (Oxford: Basic Blackwell, 1977).

Vanderpoel, Emily Noyes, *Color Problems: A Practical Manual for the Lay Student of Color* (New York, London, Bombay: Longmans, Green & Co., 1902).

Vanherman, T. H., *Every Man his Own House-painter and Colourman, the Whole Forming a Complete System for the Amelioration of the Noxious Quality of Common Paint; a Number of Invaluable Inventions, Discoveries and Improvements, and a Variety of Other Particulars that Relate to the House-painting in General* (London: I. F. Setchel; Simpkin and Marshall; and J. Booth, 1829).

Varley, John, *J. Varley's List of Colours* (London: J. Varley, 1818).
———*Varley's Specimens of Permanent Colours* (London: J. Varley, 1850).

Villalobos-Domínguez, Cándido and Julio Villalobos, *Atlas de los Colores/Colour Atlas*; translated by Aubrey Malyn Homer (Buenos Aires: El Ateneo Editorial, 1947).

Voltaire, *Elémens de la philosophie de Neuton/mis à la portée de tout le monde, par Mr. de Voltaire* (Amsterdam: Chez Jacques Desbordes, 1738).

Waller, Richard, 'A Catalogue of Simple and Mixt Colours, with a Specimen of each Colour prefixt to its proper Name', in *Philosophical Transactions of the Royal Society of London* Vol. 16, 1686.

Warren, Henry, *Hints Upon Tints, with Strokes Upon Copper and Canvass* (London: printed for J.F. Setchel, 1833).

Werner, Abraham Gottlob, *Von den äusserlichen Kennzeichen der Fossilien* (Leipzig: Crusius, 1774).

Wilkinson, Sir John Gardner, *On Colour and the necessity for a General Diffusion of Taste among all Classes* (London: John Murray, 1858).

Wilson, Robert Arthur, *The Colour Circle, Based Upon Nature (The Rainbow) and Hand-Coloured* (UK, privately published, no date, *c.* 1920s).

Wilson, Robert Francis, *Colour and Light at Work* (London: Seven Oaks Press, 1953).
———*The Wilson Colour Chart*, (London: British Colour Council, *c.* 1938).

Index

A
Ackermann, Rudolph 40, 65, 74, 186
acrylic paints 204
Adam, Edouard 195
additive colours 15, 24, 27, 61, 144
aesthetics 7, 13, 15, 30, 32
   nineteenth century 39, 46, 121, 130
   twentieth century 137, 166, 182, 191
Albers, Josef 138
Allen, Edward Prascey 35
Allen, Sam 210, 214
Amenemope, Vizier 7
Apollinaire, Guillame 156
aquatinting 8, 68, 74, 78, 87
Armstrong, John 184
ARoS Aarhus Kunstmuseum 221 223
Art Nouveau 170, 174
Auerbach, Tauba 144
auras 137, 160

B
Baretti, Joseph 20
Barnard, George 106, 108, 138
baroque 20
Barrett Carpenter, Henry 147
Bartolozzi, Francesco 20, 36
Batchelor, David 197, 224
Baty, Patrick 193, 208
Baty, Robert 208
Baudelaire, Charles 124
Bauhaus 8, 135, 137, 160, 162, 172, 174–176, 180, 182, 193
Baxter, George 106
Baynard Press 186
Bell, Vanessa 184
Benson, William 87, 118, 121, 144
Besant, Annie 160
Birren, Faber 24, 168
Blanc, Charles 122, 224
Der Blaue Reiter 135, 137, 164, 170
Bloch, Albert 164
Bloomsbury Group 184
Böcklin, Arnold 155
Boutet, Claude 17–18, 50
Boydell, Josiah 36
Brewster, David 108
British Colour Council 137, 199
Brough, Jack 197
Brown, Lancelot 'Capability' 46
Brutalism 193
Burke, Edmund 27, 30
Burnet, John 54, 68

C
Callahan, Tyree 220
Campbell, Richard 35
Castel, Louis Bertrand 66
Cawse, John 68, 70
Cennini, Cennino 104
Centre Georges Pompidou 193
Cerrini, Giovanni Domenico 20
Cézanne, Paul 129, 170
Chevreul, Michel Éugène 45, 87–88, 90–92, 94, 96, 100, 102, 108, 118, 130, 138, 142, 147, 156, 221
chroma 140
Chromatic Process 106
chromo-luminarism 100
chromolithography 116
chromophobia 224
CIELAB 142, 191
Clarke, Charles 48
Classicism 39
Cleland, T. M. 142
CMYK model 144, 193
coal-tar 112–113
cold colours 46, 54, 204
Cologne Cathedral 214
colour 1–9
   cold colours 46, 54, 204
   colour balls 151
   colour blots 50, 78, 108, 138
   colour categories 102
   colour cubes 87, 118, 144
   colour dials 209
   colour globes 8, 118, 140, 142, 144, 176
   colour grids 138, 214
   colour harmony 7–8, 20, 32, 39, 46, 50, 61, 66, 78, 83, 92, 104, 106, 116–117, 138, 147–148, 166, 170, 172, 176, 195, 204, 207
   colour memorandums 48
   colour space 140, 144, 191
   colour spheres 140, 176, 180
   colour squares 138, 180
   colour stars 46, 61, 65–66, 176, 180, 204
   colour stops 188
   colour trees 140, 142, 144
   warm colours 46, 48, 54, 82, 204
colour circles 17, 61, 72
   nineteenth century 87, 91, 96, 130
   twentieth century 144, 147, 172, 180, 221, 223
colour plates 46, 48, 50, 66
   nineteenth century 68, 72, 74, 78, 90–92, 94, 96, 102, 106, 108, 113–114, 116–118, 121, 130
   twentieth century 137–138, 142, 147–148, 151–152, 155, 160, 168, 180, 182, 184, 188, 199–200
colour theory 8, 11, 15, 17
   eighteenth century 20, 23–24, 27, 30
   nineteenth century 39–40, 42, 45–46, 66, 72, 83, 88, 91, 100, 102, 104, 106, 116–118, 121–122, 130
   twentieth century 135, 137, 144, 147–148, 151, 153, 155–156, 159, 162, 166, 168, 172, 174, 176, 180, 184, 195, 200, 207, 224
colour wheels 8, 11, 13–15
   eighteenth century 17–18, 27
   nineteenth century 45–46, 50, 61, 66, 72, 92, 96, 121
   twentieth century 135, 144, 147–148, 155–156, 159, 166, 168–169, 176, 190, 193, 197, 199, 204, 207, 216, 218, 221
colourmen 35, 61, 65, 87, 104, 155, 199
Commission internationale de l'éclairage 191
complementary colours 46, 83, 108, 118, 121–122, 138, 152, 166, 176, 184, 207
Constructivism 160
copperplate engraving 11, 27, 42, 54, 87, 137
Coventry Cathedral 210, 214
Cox, David 54
Crace, John Gregory 45
Cubism 135, 156
Curwen, Harold 197
Curwen, John 197
Curwen Press 197
cut-outs 148, 188
cyanometers 216

D
Da Vinci, Leonardo 54, 72, 138, 159, 166
Daler-Rowney 35
Darwin, Charles 56
Daughters of the American Revolution 138
Dawe, Gabriel 220–221
Day & Son 87, 114, 186
De Lemos, Pedro Joseph 148, 151
De Saussure, Horace-Bénédict 216
Degas, Edgar 88, 126
Delacroix, Éugène 124, 126
Delaunay, Robert 15, 156, 170
Delaunay, Sonia 15, 156
Deluge paintings 82–83
Derain, André 135
Diesbach, Heinrich 11
Digeon, René-Henri 87, 96

digital colour 8, 172, 180, 195, 214
dimensionality 92, 140, 144, 164, 174, 176, 204, 224
Dippel, Johann Konrad 11
Divisionism 100
Doesburg, Theo van 174
Doric mode 15
Dossie, Robert 30
Duveneck, Frank 155

E
Eastlake, Charles Lock 42, 45, 83, 85
Eiermann, Egon 214
electromagnetic radiation 15
Eliasson, Olafur 8, 220–221, 223
enamel paints 208
Enlightenment 13, 15, 27, 39
Expressionism 7, 135, 138, 160, 170, 174

F
Faber and Faber 186
Faraday, Michael 106
Farington, Joseph 36
Les Fauves 135
Fauvism 135
Feininger, Lyonel 164, 174
De Fem 159
Field, George 45, 61, 65–66, 83, 87, 104, 108, 138, 155
Fielding, Theodore Henry 68
Finch, Spencer 216
First World War 170, 182
Fischer, Martin 155
fluorescence 118
fold-outs 188, 208
Foster, Walter T. 204, 207
Futurism 156

G
Gage, John 45, 83
garden colour 46
Gardiner, T. 50
Gartside, Mary 50, 61, 78, 104, 108, 138, 144
Giacometti, Alberto 50
Gillray, James 36
Gilpin, William 32–33
Giotto 116
Glaesener, Jürgen 172
Gloag, John 182
Goethe, Johann Wolfgang von 20, 39, 42, 45, 50, 61, 65, 82–83, 85, 91, 102, 108, 135, 137–138, 159–160, 162, 176, 184, 200, 224

gouache 65, 68, 78
Grant, Duncan 184
Graphische Anstalt E. Wartelsteiner 180
Great Exhibition 87, 104, 114
greyscale 91, 130, 142, 166
Griffits, Thomas E. 186, 188
Gropius, Walter 172, 174, 176

H
Haagen, Ernst van 176
hand-colouring 11, 17, 27
    nineteenth century 39, 46, 50, 54, 65, 68, 74, 78, 87, 92, 114
    twentieth century 137, 193
Hardie, George 218
Harris, Moses 8, 11, 27, 40, 50, 72, 83, 188
Harvard University 166
Hay, David Ramsay 46, 66
Hayter, Charles 40, 72, 83
Helmholtz, Hermann von 121, 151, 162
Hentschel, Carl 137
Herbert, Lawrence 195
Hering, Karl Ewald Konstantin 162, 166
Herschel, John 108, 118
Hipgnosis 218
Hirst, Damien 87
Hogarth, William 27, 30–31, 68, 124
Hölzel, Adolf 162, 176, 180
Hope, Thomas 200
House of Parsons 208
Howard, Frank 78, 80
hue 140, 144, 151, 156, 160, 166, 168–169, 172, 176, 199, 216, 223–224
hue, value, chroma (HVC) 140, 166
Humboldt, Alexander von 216
Hunt, William Holman 65
Hutton, John 210

I
Impressionism 87–88, 100, 121, 126–127, 129, 135, 170
Industrial Revolution 40, 87
International Klein Blue (IKB) 195
Ionides, Basil 182
Itten, Johannes 174, 176, 180

J
Jacobs, Michel 151–153
Jawlensky, Alexej von 164
Jones, Owen 87, 104, 114, 117
Jugendstil 170

K
Kaiser Wilhelm Memorial Church 214
Kandinsky, Wassily 15, 135, 137, 160, 162, 164, 170, 174, 195
Kant, Immanuel 102
Kapoor, Anish 195
Kauffman, Angelica 20, 22, 36
Keler, Peter 174
Kelm, Daniel E. 144
Kircher, Athanasius 66
Klee, Paul 135, 137, 170, 172, 174, 176, 180
Klein, Yves 195
Af Klint, Hilma 159–160
Kokoschka, Oskar 174
Kupka, Frantisek 156

L
Lacouture, Charles 130, 138
Lairesse, Gérard de 30
Lambert, Johann Heinrich 17, 184
landscapes 32, 42, 46, 48, 54, 68, 70, 100, 106, 114, 159
Laplace, M. 127
Lawrence, Thomas 78
Le Blon, Jacob Christoph 24, 68
Le Brun, Elisabeth Louise Vigée 128–129
Leadbeater, Charles Webster 137, 159–161
Leighton Brothers 106
Leighton, George Cargill 106
Leroy, Louis 88
letterpress 142, 199
lightboxes 218, 226
lithography 8, 39, 65, 68
    nineteenth century 74, 78, 87, 91–92, 102, 104, 106, 114, 118, 130
    twentieth century 147–148, 153, 155, 168, 186, 188, 221

M
M & J Levine Advertising 193
Macke, August 164
magnetism 106
Manet, Édouard 126
Marc, Franz 135, 164
Matisse, Henri 135, 180
Maugham, Syrie 184
Maxwell, James 162
Mayer, Tobias 17
Mengs, Anton Raphael 54
Meridian 210
Mérimée, Jean-François-Léonor 72
Merrifield, Mary Philadelphia 65, 87, 104, 138

metal plate engraving 11, 27, 42, 54, 87, 137
Middle Ages 7
Mies van der Rohe, Ludwig 174
Millais, John Everett 65
Miller, William 50
Milner, Isaac 46
Minimalism 137, 174, 180
MK Gallery 226
Modernism 45, 138, 159, 174, 182, 195
Moholy-Nagy, Lásló 172, 174
Mondrian, Piet 180
Monet, Claude 88, 127
Müller, Johannes Peter 45
Munsell, Albert Henry 140, 142, 144, 166, 168, 176, 191
Munsell, Alexander E.R. 142
Munsell Color Company 142
Munsell Color Foundation 142
Münter, Gabriele 7, 124, 164
music 8, 15, 45, 66, 156, 170, 172, 218
mysticism 137, 156, 159–160

N
neoclassicism 20
Newman, Barnett 195
Newton, Charles 35
Newton, Henry 65
Newton, Isaac 11–15, 17–18, 20, 23–24, 27, 30, 39, 42, 45–46, 50, 54, 66, 72, 90, 100, 117, 121, 144, 147, 156, 159, 184, 218, 220–221, 223–224
Nobel Prize 166

O
oil paints 68, 70, 78, 88, 126, 155, 204, 216
Opticks 11–15, 17, 24, 27, 30, 45
Oram, William 48, 54
Orphism 156
Ostwald, Friedrich Wilhelm 137, 142, 155, 166, 168–169, 184, 188
Oughton, Frederick 113
overlay printing 186

P
Pacific Press Publishing 148
Pantone® 144, 195, 218, 226
Pantone Color Institute 226
Pantone Matching System (PMS) 195, 226
Papers and Paints 193, 208–209
Parsons, Thomas 208–209
patents 88, 112
Patmore, Derek Coventry 184

Paxton, Joseph 104
Peel, Robert 104
Penguin 197
Perkin, William 112
phenomenology 40
photography 8, 27, 108, 126, 137, 147, 155, 160, 180, 182, 184, 193, 204, 216
Pick, Frank 188
picturesque, the 32, 46, 116
pigments 7, 11, 13, 17, 23
    eighteenth century 27, 32, 35
    nineteenth century 42, 48, 54, 56, 61, 65, 68, 87, 90, 100, 104, 106, 108, 113, 116, 121–122, 124, 127, 129
    twentieth century 135, 137, 140, 147, 152, 155, 166, 195, 197, 202, 206, 209–210, 216, 218, 226
Pink Floyd 218–219
Piot, Léon 124
Piper, John 210, 214
Pissarro, Camille 88, 127
Pointillism 100
pollution 155
Post-Impressionism 100, 121, 135, 164, 170
Poussin, Nicholas 48
Pre-Raphaelite Brotherhood 65
primary colours 7, 14, 17
    eighteenth century 20, 24, 27
    nineteenth century 54, 61, 65–66, 72, 91, 102, 106, 108, 113, 116, 118, 127, 130
    twentieth century 151, 159, 172, 174, 176, 182, 184, 197, 199, 214
primitivism 164
print culture/technology 8
    eighteenth century 11, 24
    nineteenth century 40, 46, 48, 68, 74, 87, 92, 96, 106, 113
    twentieth century 137–138, 142, 144, 147–148, 151–153, 180, 182, 186, 188, 190–191, 193, 197, 207, 226
Provis, Ann Jemima 36
Prozor, Maurice 160
Prussian Blue 11, 35, 70, 113, 195, 216
psychology 182, 184, 199–201
Puffin Picture Books 197
Pythagoras 15, 66

Q
Quarto Publishing 207

R
Rand, John Goffe 88

Reeves Brothers 35
Reeves, William 32
Renaissance 104, 135
Renoir, Auguste 88
Repton, Humphrey 46, 114, 116–117, 200
Reynolds, Joshua 13, 36
RGB model 144
Richter, Gerhard 195, 214
Riley, Bridget 195
rococo 20
Romanticism 39, 45, 124, 216
Romney, George 23
Rood, Ogden Nicholas 88, 121, 138, 147
Rothko, Mark 197
Rowney Brothers 35
Rowney, Richard 35
Rowney, Thomas 35
Royal Academy 13, 20, 36, 50, 78
Royal Academy of Fine Arts 159
Royal Horticultural Society 199
Rubens, Peter Paul 78
Runge, Philipp Otto 118, 144, 176

S
Sadler, Michael T. H. 162
saturation 14, 17, 50, 66, 140, 144, 151, 159, 176, 199
Scharf, George 35
Schiffermüller, Ignaz 17
Schiller, Friedrich 45
Schlemmer, Oskar 174
Schmid, F. 50
Schopenhauer, Arthur 45
Second World War 137, 176, 188, 193, 197, 208, 214
secondary colours 17, 27
    nineteenth century 54, 61, 72, 102, 106, 108, 113, 118, 127
    twentieth century 159, 172, 174, 176, 197
Semple, Stuart 195
Senefelder, Alois 74, 184
Seurat, Georges 100, 135
Siedhogg-Buscher, Alma 174
silkscreen-printing 8, 180
Smithsonian American Art Museum 221
Sol, J.C.M. 102
Sowerby, James 61
Spectro-Matic Colour Dispenser 202
spectrophotometers 190
spectrum 7, 11, 14–15, 23
    eighteenth century 30
    nineteenth century 42, 50, 82, 94, 96, 117,

121
  twentieth century 144, 151–153, 156, 190, 210, 218, 220–221, 223–224
Spence, Basil 193, 210–211, 214
Spiller, Jürg 172
Spink, Gertrude 160
Steiner, Rudolph 159–160
De Stijl 166
Stokes, George Gabriel 118
Strathmore Paper Company 142
sublime palettes 30, 32, 39
subtractive colours 24, 27, 61, 91, 144, 193
Sussex University 210, 214
symbolism 61, 170
Syme, Patrick 56, 59
synaesthesia 15, 66, 174

T
Taylor, J. Scott 168
Temperament Rose, the 45, 137
tertiary colours 17, 30, 61, 106, 108, 113, 127, 172
tetrachromatic system 20, 24, 54, 72, 166
Theosophical Society 137, 159–160
Thomas Parsons & Sons 208
Thorgerson, Storm 218
Titian 36, 78, 80
trichromatic system 24, 32, 61, 91, 147–148, 162, 174, 209
Turner, Joseph Mallord William 42, 78, 81–83, 85, 138, 221

U
University of Cambridge 14
University of Metz 130

value 140, 207
Van Gogh, Theo 120
Van Gogh, Vincent 122, 124, 135, 164, 170
Vanderpoel, Emily Noyes 137–138
Vantablack 195
Vauquelin, Louis Nicolas 90
Vauxcelles, Louis 135
Venetian colouring 36
Villalobos, Julio 190
Villalobos-Dominguez, Candido 190

W
Walter Carson & Sons 202
Walter Foster Publishing 204, 207
Waring & Dimes 35
warm colours 46, 48, 54, 82, 204

watercolours 13, 17, 23, 32
  eighteenth century 35
  nineteenth century 40, 50, 54, 65, 68, 74, 78, 106, 117, 121
  twentieth century 155, 170, 204, 216
wavelengths 15, 121, 218
Werefkin, Marianne von 7, 164
Werner, Abraham Gottlob 56, 59
West & Co 114
West, Benjamin 20, 36
Whistler, James Abbott McNeill 155
Wilberforce, William 46
Wilkinson, John Gardner 114, 116–117, 138
Wilson Colour Chart 166, 199
Wilson, Robert Arthur 8
Wilson, Robert Francis 199–201
Winsor & Newton 35, 65, 88, 104, 168
Winsor, William 35, 65
Wittgenstein, Ludwig 45
woodblock prints/woodcuts 11
  nineteenth century 42, 74, 87, 106, 121
  twentieth century 137, 142, 148, 162, 193

Y
Yale University Press 180
Young, Thomas 121, 151, 162

Picture Credits

With special thanks to the **Colour Reference Library, Royal College of Art, London**, Photography by Clive Boursnell *12–13, 25, 26, 28–29, 38, 41, 43, 66, 73 above and below, 84–85, 86, 90–91, 92, 93 above and below, 94–95, 97–99, 103, 118, 119 above and below, 120, 131, 132–133, 138, 139, 140, 141 above and below, 145, 162, 163, 190, 191, 198.*

Additional picture credits:

Alamy Stock Photo *Classic Image 30; Granger Historical Picture Archive 129; Heritage Image Partnership Ltd. 165; Ivy Close Images 128; Peter Horree 156.* **akg-images** *44; Bildarchiv Steffens 215 below.* **Alexandra Loske** *142, 202, 203, 215 above.* **Bibliothèque de Genève** *216.* **Bridgeman Images** *© British Library Board. All Rights Reserved 18, 19; Courtesy of the Warden and Scholars of New College, Oxford 15; Haags Gemeentemuseum, The Hague, Netherlands 158; Hamburger Kunsthalle, Hamburg, Germany 144; Jeu de Paume, Paris, France 122; Kunstmuseum, Basel, Switzerland/Gift of Richard Doetsch-Benziger, 1960 171; Louvre, Paris, France/De Agostini Picture Library/G. Dagli Orti 126; National Portrait Gallery, London, UK/Photo © Stefano Baldini 31; Philadelphia Museum of Art, Pennsylvania, PA, USA/The Louise and Walter Arensberg Collection, 1950. © ADAGP, Paris and DACS, London 2017 157; Private Collection 164; Private Collection. © The Joseph and Anni Albers Foundation/VG Bild-Kunst, Bonn and DACS, London 2017 181; Sterling and Francine Clark Art Institute, Williamstown, Massachusetts, USA 127.* **Courtesy of the Josef and Anni Albers Foundation** *180.* **Courtesy Sam Allen**, *photo by Clive Boursnell 210.* © **David Batchelor** *225, photo by Marcus Leith 224.* © **Gabriel Dawe**, *Plexus A1, 2015, Renwick Gallery of the Smithsonian American Art Museum, Courtesy Conduit Gallery. Photo by Ron Blunt 221.* **Getty Images** *Hulton Archive 35; Science & Society Picture Library 23 right.* **Getty Research Institute** *16.* **Jim Pike** *47, 74, 75.* **National Gallery of Art Washington**, *Collection of Mr. and Mrs. Paul Mellon 100.* © **Olafur Eliasson**, *Photo by Jens Ziehe, Berlin; Courtesy the artist; Tanya Bonakdar Gallery, New York 223, Photo by Ole Hein Pedersen; Courtesy the artist; ARoS Aarhus Kunstmuseum 222 above, Photo by Thilo Frank, Studio Olafur Eliasson; Courtesy the artist; ARoS Aarhus Kunstmuseum 222 below.* **Penguin Random House UK**, *cover design © Penguin Books Ltd., 1948, reproduced by permission of Penguin Random House UK 196.* **Photo by Clive Boursnell**, *used with permission of David Gilmour, Nick Mason, Roger Waters and the Richard Wright Estate 219.* **REX Shutterstock** *British Library/Robana 7 below.* © **RMN**-*Grand Palais (musée du Louvre) / Hervé Lewandowski 125.* **Royal Academy of Arts, London**; *Photographer: John Hammond 22.* © **Spencer Finch** *217.* **Strat Mastoris** *34, 175 above.* **SuperStock** *3LH 123.* **Tate Images** *Digital Image © Tate, London 2014 89; Digital Image © Tate, London 2014, © 1998 Kate Rothko Prizel & Christopher Rothko ARS, NY and DACS, London 194; Digital Image © Tate, London 2014, © Succession Henri Matisse / DACS 2018 134; Digital Image © Tate, London 2017 82, 83.* **Tecta** *175 below.* © **The Trustees of the British Museum** *37.* **Tyree Callahan** *220.* **Universitatsbibliothek Heidelberg** *via CC licence 54. Wikimedia Commons public domain 17, 21.* **www.kettererkunst.com** *© DACS 2017 6.* **Yale Center for British Art**, *Paul Mellon Collection 33.* **Zentrum Paul Klee** *173.*

Right: Artist Eva Bodinet's colour globe, made from a traditional cardboard globe overlaid with strips of paper painted with acrylic paint.

PICTURE CREDITS 239

Acknowledgements

For their support, both personal and professional, and inspiration through the years I would like to thank:

All my friends and colleagues at the University of Sussex, the Royal Pavilion and Brighton Museums, the Arts and Humanities Research Counci, the Attingham Trust, the Yale Center for British Art, the Colour Reference Library at the Royal College of Art, the National Art Library at the V&A, the British Library, The Keep Archives in East Sussex, and, especially, Tracy Anderson, Mark Aronson, Kevin Bacon, David Batchelor, Patrick Baty, David Beevers, Andrew Bennett, Meskerem Berhane, Clare Best, Carole Biggam, Eva Bodinet, Clarisse Bourgeois, Clive Boursnell, Philip Bradley, Janet Brough, Franky Bulmer, Meaghan Clarke, Nicola Coleby, Patrick Conner, Fiona Courage, Steve Creffield, Neil Cunningham, Jessica David, Stuart Durant, Olafur Eliasson, Kate Elms, Jenny Gaschke, Sarah Gibbings, Gordon Grant, Fergus Hare, Maurice Howard, Carl Jennings, Colin and Rose Jones, Renate Klauck-Neils, Simon Lane, Zara Larcombe, Ric Latham, Robin Lee, Carol Lewis, Flora Loske-Page, Jenny Lund, Chris McDermott, Erwin Paul Mark, David J Markham, Robert Massey, Tamsin and Strat Mastoris, Jonathan Menezes, Jochen Menge, Peter Messer, Shona Milton, Klaus Neils, Michelle O'Malley, Patrick Marrin, Roy Osborne, Jeremy Page, Neil Parkinson, Steve Pavey, Jim Pike, Matthew Platts, Sarah Posey, Geoff Quilley, Rupert Radcliffe-Genge, Hazel Rayner, Jacqueline Rietz, Linda Rossbach, Jae Jennifer Rossman, Rachel Silverlight, Abraham Thomas, Lindy Usher, Jennifer Veall, Ian Warrell, Marianne Wiehn, and Chandra Wohleber.